# Mixing and Mastering with Pro Tools 11

To access online media visit:
**www.halleonard.com/mylibrary**

Enter Code
8198-7931-7733-1270

## quick**PRO**
### guides

# MIXING AND MASTERING WITH PRO TOOLS 11

Glenn Lorbecki and Greg "Stryke" Chin

HAL•LEONARD®

An Imprint of Hal Leonard Corporation

Published in 2014 by Hal Leonard Books
An Imprint of Hal Leonard Corporation
7777 West Bluemound Road
Milwaukee, WI 53213

Trade Book Division Editorial Offices
33 Plymouth St., Montclair, NJ 07042

Printed in the United States of America

Book design by Adam Fulrath
Book composition by Rainbow Tiger Design and Bill Gibson

Library of Congress Cataloging-in-Publication Data

Lorbecki, Glenn.
 Mixing and mastering with Pro Tools 11 / Glenn Lorbecki and Greg "Stryke" Chin.
    pages cm
Includes index.
1. Pro Tools. 2. Digital audio editors. 3. Mastering (Sound recordings) I. Stryke (Musician)
II. Title.
ML74.4.P76L673 2014
781.3'4536--dc23
                          2014028528


ISBN 978-1-4803-5509-5

www.halleonardbooks.com

To my beautiful children, Evan and Erika
—Glenn

For my wife, Amanda
—Greg

# CONTENTS

Preface ...................................................................................... xiii
Acknowledgments ..................................................................... xv

## Introduction

**Pro Tools Primer** ........................................................................1
    What's New in Pro Tools 11? ............................................................ 1
        Digidesign Is Now AVID................................................................ 2
        Drag and Drop Installation ........................................................... 2
        64-Bit Architecture ...................................................................... 2
        AAX Plug-in Support .................................................................... 2
        DAE Is Dead, Long Live AAE ........................................................ 2
        Aggregate I/O ............................................................................. 2
        Dual Audio Buffers ...................................................................... 2
        Offline Bounce............................................................................. 2
        Advanced Metering....................................................................... 3
        Avid Video Engine ....................................................................... 3
        Insert Bypass Shortcuts................................................................. 3
        New Automation Features.............................................................. 3
        New Workspace Browser................................................................ 3
        Satellite Technology ..................................................................... 3
        GUI Improvements........................................................................ 3
        Session Import/Export .................................................................. 3
    What Should You Bring to the Party?................................................ 4
    How to Use This Book and Related Online Materials ......................... 4
        Video ......................................................................................... 5
        Session Data and Audio Files ........................................................ 5
        Additional Materials..................................................................... 5
        Updates....................................................................................... 6

## Chapter 1

**What Makes a Good Mix?** ........................................................... 7
    Do Not Confuse a Good Mix with a "Good Song" ............................. 7
        A Great Song vs. a Great Mix........................................................ 8
        What Makes a Bad Mix? ............................................................... 8
        Think Like a Mixer vs. a Tracking Engineer .................................. 8
        Basic Mixing Tools ...................................................................... 8
        Volume-Based Tools..................................................................... 9
        Time-Based Tools......................................................................... 9
        Spatial Effects ............................................................................. 9
        Analog vs. Digital Workflow......................................................... 9
        Creative Language vs. Technical Language.................................... 10
    Studio Basics: Control Room Environment/Acoustics.................... 10
        Pro Studios ............................................................................... 10

## Contents

Project Studios .................................................................................11

Home Studios ..................................................................................11

Equipment ...........................................................................................11

Computers ......................................................................................12

Audio Hard Drives ........................................................................12

Mixing Consoles ............................................................................13

Outboard Hardware Processing ....................................................13

Control Surfaces ............................................................................13

Monitoring......................................................................................14

Listening Styles .............................................................................14

Format Information ........................................................................15

Chapter 1 Review.................................................................................15

## Chapter 2

## The Pro Tools System .............................................................................17

Software Overview ...............................................................................17

Hardware Overview: Two Modes........................................................17

1. Pro Tools ....................................................................................18

2. Pro Tools HD.............................................................................18

Outboard Gear ..............................................................................19

iLok ................................................................................................20

System Calibration ..............................................................................20

Optimizing the Pro Tools Environment.......................................20

System Usage Window ..................................................................20

Playback Engine ............................................................................21

Buffer Settings ..............................................................................21

Host Processors .............................................................................21

Delay Compensation Engine........................................................22

Dynamic Plug-in Processing.........................................................22

Cache Size .....................................................................................22

Apply Changes ..............................................................................22

Very Important Note!.....................................................................22

Hardware Settings .........................................................................22

Peripherals ....................................................................................22

Sample Rate ...................................................................................23

Clock Source..................................................................................23

Optical Format ..............................................................................23

Launch Setup App.........................................................................23

Disk Allocation .............................................................................23

I/O Settings....................................................................................23

Handy Pro Tools Functions.................................................................24

Edit Modes ....................................................................................24

Edit Tools ......................................................................................25

Pro Tools Conventions..................................................................26

Key Commands .............................................................................26

Keyboard Focus.............................................................................26

Summary of Key Commands ..............................................................28

Chapter 2 Review.................................................................................28

## Chapter 3

**Managing Your Virtual Studio** ...................................................................**31**

    Configuring a Virtual Mixer in Pro Tools.................................................31

        Tracks...................................................................................................31

        Stereo Pan Depth.................................................................................32

        Groups.................................................................................................32

        Sub-Masters.........................................................................................33

        Aux Sends/Returns..............................................................................33

        Inserts..................................................................................................33

        Sends...................................................................................................38

        Master Faders......................................................................................40

        Clearing Clipped Signal Indicators.....................................................41

        Dither...................................................................................................41

        Turning up the HEAT—

           Harmonically Enhanced Algorithm Technology ...........................41

        Organizing Your Tracks.......................................................................43

        Edit Window Layout............................................................................44

        Grid Settings.......................................................................................46

        Nudge Settings....................................................................................46

        Color Palette........................................................................................47

        Memory Locations/Markers.................................................................47

        Window Configurations.......................................................................50

        Transport Window...............................................................................53

    Editing Operations ....................................................................................53

        Playlists................................................................................................53

        Duplicating Tracks..............................................................................54

        Cleaning Tracks...................................................................................55

        Strip Silence........................................................................................55

        Noise Gates.........................................................................................55

        Manual Editing....................................................................................56

        Mute Clip vs. Cut and Remove...........................................................56

        Consolidating Clips.............................................................................56

    Summary of Key Commands......................................................................57

    Chapter 3 Review.......................................................................................58

## Chapter 4

**Mixing Tools** .......................................................................................**59**

    Audio Suite Plug-ins .................................................................................59

    Working with Plug-in Inserts .....................................................................59

        AAX—Avid Audio eXtension (Native) ................................................59

        AAX—Avid Audio eXtension (DSP) ....................................................60

        Inserting a Plug-in on Your Track.......................................................60

        To View Multiple Plug-in Windows.....................................................60

        Plug-in Manipulation..........................................................................60

        Copying Plug-in Settings.....................................................................61

        The Secret of the Right Mouse-Click..................................................61

        Printing Tracks with Real-Time Plug-in Effects .................................62

        Side-Chain Effects...............................................................................62

Processing Tools for Your Toolkit..................................................................62
Frequency Tools............................................................................................63
    EQ..............................................................................................................63
    Harmonic Enhancement..........................................................................66
Dynamic Range Control..............................................................................66
    Compression/Limiting.............................................................................66
    Multi-Band Compression.........................................................................67
    Expanders/Noise Gates............................................................................67
    De-Essers...................................................................................................67
Pitch Tools.....................................................................................................68
    Pitch Change.............................................................................................68
    Pitch Correction.......................................................................................68
    Creative Use of Pitch Effects....................................................................69
Time-Based Effects.......................................................................................69
    Phase-Reverse...........................................................................................69
    Reverb.......................................................................................................70
    Delay.........................................................................................................70
    Modulation Effects...................................................................................70
    Time Compression/Expansion, or TC/E..................................................71
Other Effects.................................................................................................71
    Distortion..................................................................................................71
    Other Tools and Plug-ins.........................................................................71
Summary of Key Commands.........................................................................72
Chapter 4 Review..........................................................................................73

## Chapter 5

**Understanding Automation** ...................................................... **75**
Quick-Start Guide to Automation.................................................................75
Track Parameters That Can Be Automated....................................................76
    Audio Track Parameters...........................................................................76
    Auxiliary Input Track Parameters............................................................76
    Master Fader Parameters..........................................................................76
    MIDI Track Parameters............................................................................76
    Instrument Track Parameters...................................................................76
Recording Real-Time Automation................................................................76
    Automation Modes...................................................................................76
    Enabling Automation...............................................................................77
    Performing an Automation Pass...............................................................77
    Plug-in Automation..................................................................................78
    Auto Safe Mode........................................................................................78
    Viewing and Editing Automation Data....................................................78
    Thinning Automation...............................................................................79
    Strategies for Automating Your Mix.........................................................79
    Working with Control Surfaces.................................................................80
    AVID C|24................................................................................................80
    EuCon.......................................................................................................80
Summary of Key Commands.........................................................................82
Chapter 5 Review..........................................................................................82

## Chapter 6

**The Art and Science of the Mix** .......................................................... **83**
  The Weakest Link—Recording Quality vs. Final Results ............................... 83
  Musical Styles/Genres .................................................................................... 83
  Editing for Content ........................................................................................ 84
  Mixing "In the Box" vs. Mixing on a Console ................................................ 84
  Tracksheets/Documentation ......................................................................... 84
  Keeping Track of Mix Sessions and Mix Files .............................................. 85
  Naming Conventions ...................................................................................... 85
  Data Management .......................................................................................... 85
  Keep an Eye on the Final Delivery Medium .................................................. 86
  P&E DAW Session Guidelines Document ..................................................... 86
  P&E Master Delivery Document ................................................................... 86
    P&E Wing ..................................................................................................... 86
  Basic Approaches to Mixing ......................................................................... 86
  Building a House (of *Rock*) ........................................................................... 87
    Drums .......................................................................................................... 87
    Bass ............................................................................................................. 93
    Guitar (GTR) ............................................................................................... 95
    Keyboard Tracks ........................................................................................ 96
    Other Instruments ..................................................................................... 97
    Vocals .......................................................................................................... 98
  Sculpting a Mix ............................................................................................. 98
  Technical Aspects .......................................................................................... 99
    Dynamic Range ........................................................................................... 99
    Gain Structure ............................................................................................ 99
    Frequency Response .................................................................................. 100
    Metering ..................................................................................................... 100
    Mixing to a Digital File ............................................................................. 101
  Mixing Summary ........................................................................................... 103
  Preparing Your Tracks for Mastering ......................................................... 103
  Summary of Key Commands ........................................................................ 104
  Chapter 6 Review ......................................................................................... 104

## Chapter 7

**The Mastering Overview** ...................................................................... **105**
  What Does a Mastering Engineer Do? .......................................................... 105
    When Do You Need Mastering? ................................................................ 105
    You Should Have Your Music Mastered If ............................................... 106
    Should You Master Your Own Mixes? ..................................................... 106
    Thinking Like a Mastering Engineer vs. a Mixing Engineer .................... 106
  Basic Mastering Tools .................................................................................. 107
    Volume-Based Effects ................................................................................ 107
    Time-Based Effects .................................................................................... 107
    Reconstructive Tools ................................................................................. 107
  Mastering in Pro Tools ................................................................................. 107
    What You *Can* Do In Pro Tools .............................................................. 107

# Contents

What You *Can't* Do in Pro Tools ............................................................................107
Pro Tools in the Mastering Suite ...........................................................................108
DIY Mastering in Pro Tools ...................................................................................108
Building a Mastering Session .................................................................................109
Assembling Tracks...................................................................................................109
Monitoring................................................................................................................109
Signal Chain.............................................................................................................109
Using Level Automation ........................................................................................110
Dynamic Range Control.........................................................................................110
Parallel Compression ..............................................................................................110
Serial Compression..................................................................................................111
Using More Than One Compressor on a Track...................................................111
Multi-Band Compression........................................................................................111
Restorative Use of Multi-Band Compression......................................................111
EQ..............................................................................................................................111
Create a Master Fader.............................................................................................112
Create A Pre- and Post-Processing Monitor Bus.................................................112
Overall Level Optimization.....................................................................................112
The Level Wars ........................................................................................................113
Checklist Before Printing Final Bounces .............................................................113
Bouncing Your Mastered Files...............................................................................113
Creating the Final Master CD ................................................................................114
Do I Need to Master My Music for MP3 Distribution? .....................................114
Documentation.........................................................................................................115
Delivering a Master for Duplication .....................................................................115
Delivering a Master for Online Distribution........................................................115
Backup vs. Long-Term Archival of Your Data .....................................................115
Mastering Summary ...............................................................................................116
Summary of Key Commands ...............................................................................116
Chapter 7 Review....................................................................................................116
In Closing .................................................................................................................116
Frequency Chart......................................................................................................117

**Appendix: Online Video Tutorials and Pro Tools Sessions..........119**

**Answer Key for Chapter Review Questions ...................................123**

**Index......................................................................................................127**

**Credits...................................................................................................135**

# PREFACE

Welcome to the second edition of *Mixing and Mastering with Pro Tools 11*! Whether you're new to the engineer's chair or an experienced knob twister, this book will guide you through the process of mixing and mastering on one of the most powerful DAW platforms in the world—AVID Pro Tools.

This latest version of Pro Tools builds on the solid platform established and refined by AVID/Digidesign over the last twenty years, and is used by the most successful and creative engineers in the business to create the music we love so well. Pro Tools has become the de facto standard for music production and audio post-production for visual media, and you will find it in virtually every major recording facility and project studio around the world. Because of this ubiquity, it is to the advantage of every serious engineer to learn this platform thoroughly in order to get the most from your sessions. Whether you're working at home or trading files with someone across the globe, Pro Tools is a complete production environment for recording, mixing, and mastering music at the highest professional standard of quality.

Before we get started, we should outline our goals: if your aim is to arm yourself with the tools you need to be more effective at mixing and mastering music, then we are in complete harmony. The goal of this book is to get you familiar with the concepts of mixing and mastering, what it takes to create professional quality mixes, how to finish a project at the mastering stage, and how to do all of this within the Pro Tools environment. These are complex tasks, and you will need to commit a fair amount of time to learn all the techniques required to become proficient. If you put in the effort—and use this book as a guide—you will be turning out mixes that sound better than ever before.

Enjoy the ride!

# ACKNOWLEDGMENTS

Writing a book is one of the things I never thought I'd actually get to accomplish in my life. My entire career has been devoted to music, and as I've gotten little older (but not necessarily wiser), I've had the opportunity to expand that career in so many ways. While I love writing and performing music as an artist, producer, and a DJ, I also love speaking to audiences as a representative for Avid and others. Assisting in the writing of this book has been one of the highlights of my career. I would like to thank Glenn Lorbecki and Bill Gibson for asking me to be a part of this project. Your belief in me and your guidance has been absolutely essential! I'd also like to thank and acknowledge my fellow team members and friends at Avid, led by the incomparable Gil Gowing.

I have the honor of working alongside some of the best and sharpest minds in the industry. Thanks for all the knowledge you and the rest of the team have imparted to me during my time there. Thanks to you all! I hope you all enjoy reading and using this book as much as I have enjoyed working on it. —Greg

I must acknowledge those who make it possible for me to pursue my passion and to present in this book some of the experience and knowledge I've gained. Bill Gibson has stepped forward to give me the opportunity to write this book, and others, for Hal Leonard Books. Greg "Stryke" Chin has brought his intimate knowledge of the platform to this series, and I've enjoyed our collaboration!

To the many engineers, producers, musicians, and directors I've worked with over the years, I offer my humble thanks, as I've learned something from each and every one of you. You've given me tools for my toolbox and arrows for my quiver, targets to shoot for, and obstacles to avoid. We build on the knowledge and accomplishments of those who preceded us. It is my sincere hope that this book might provide some enlightenment and, perhaps, inspiration for the next wave of music makers.

I would like to acknowledge some other kind people for their assistance in this process: Kisha Kalahiki, James Nixon, and the great Bob Ludwig, with whom I co-chaired the Recording Academy Producers & Engineers Wing for five years.

Let's not forget Keely Whitney (www.KeelyWhitney.com) for the use of her wonderful music, the Mahavishnu Orchestra for the endless inspiration, and of course, AVID. —Glenn

# Introduction

# Pro Tools Primer

J ob 1 is getting your Pro Tools system up and running properly. If you already have Pro Tools 11 installed, then you're ahead of the game, and can skip past the "What's New" section if you like. If you are using Version 9 or earlier, you should read the next section, as it will give you a quick overview of what's new and what to expect.

It is critically important that you follow all of the instructions in the software and hardware installation guides that come with your Pro Tools system purchase. This book can help guide you through system settings and configuration, but the installation of your particular software modules and hardware I/O is unique to you, so you should always refer to the "Getting Started" guides and "Read Me" files in order to get your Digital Audio Workstation (DAW) up and running. Once you have the basic system operating properly, use this book as a guide to fine-tune system performance and get the most out of your Pro Tools configuration.

If you encounter problems with the initial installation of your software or hardware, you should visit (and bookmark) the section of the AVID audio forums website dedicated to addressing up-to-the-minute changes and "known issues." This is referred to as the *Digi User Conference*, or *DUC*; the website URL is http://duc.avid.com/

There is nothing more frustrating than having computer issues while trying to get up to speed on new software. While Pro Tools is equally at home on both OS X and Windows 7 and 8 platforms, you still need to have a machine with sufficient RAM, disk space, and data I/O ports. It's important to check your computer's specifications to be sure they are compatible with the current release of Pro Tools software. See the "Studio Basics" chapter of this book to determine if your computer is compatible and capable of running the software according to AVID specs. There is also a list of supported OS versions maintained on the AVID website.

## What's New in Pro Tools 11?

Since the last major upgrade to Pro Tools, the folks at Digi have been working on an upgrade that revolutionizes the way we look at buying audio workstation software and hardware. The upgrades are numerous, and we can't possibly cover them all in the scope of this book, but we will certainly delve into the changes that deal directly with mixing and mastering. Let's take a look at what's new . . .

## Digidesign Is Now AVID

AVID has owned Digi since 1995, and 2010 marked the emergence of AVID as the sole brand identity for all their audio and video software and hardware lines. As a result, the Digidesign brand name has been phased out. However, the Pro Tools name lives on, as does its reputation for being the industry standard for professional audio production. Now let's take a brief look at some of the new features of AVID's Pro Tools 11 that will have an impact on the way we work.

## Drag and Drop Installation

Installation of the Pro Tools software is much simpler with the drag and drop software installer.

## 64-Bit Architecture

Pro Tools 11 software code has been rewritten from the ground up as a 64-bit program, which means increased memory space, support for huge, complex sessions, and support for RAM-intensive virtual instruments.

## AAX Plug-in Support

AVID's new hybrid AAX plug-in format operates in both HDX accelerated DSP mode and Native mode. This replaces the older HDTDM and RTAS plug-in formats, which will no longer be supported.

## DAE Is Dead, Long Live AAE

The Digidesign Audio Engine (DAE) has been replaced by the AVID Audio Engine (AAE), allowing you to unleash the power of your host computer for processing audio. Users will see dramatic performance improvements whether using HDX or Native processing. The new AAE supports dynamic plug-in processing, whereby your system allocates system resources only when audio program is present, thereby preserving precious processing power and increasing plug-in counts systemwide.

## Aggregate I/O

This is where all of your I/O hardware comes together to create the ultimate in system flexibility. You will be able to hook up your audio interfaces all at once. The new Pro Tools audio engine allows you to connect and select from your list of I/O options, in many cases without having to restart Pro Tools.

## Dual Audio Buffers

Pro Tools uses a low-latency buffer for record and input channels, and a fixed high buffer size for playback tracks. This allows Native system users to record new session tracks with minimum delay, even while playing back existing tracks.

## Offline Bounce

Finally—you can bounce mixes using faster-than-real-time mix delivery. This is *huge*. You can also create multiple mixes simultaneously using faster-than-real-time bounce.

Gobbler users: with a mouse click, you can upload audio mixes to the cloud in Pro Tools.

## Advanced Metering

Tired of viewing peak meters? Pro Tools 11 now offers 17 different professional standard scale and ballistic settings for your session metering needs (HD version). Inserts show mini level meters for each plug-in, and gain reduction metering appears beside regular meters on channels using dynamics plug-ins. Output meters are now visible in the toolbar.

## Avid Video Engine

A newly redesigned video engine uses the same core engine as Media Composer. You can now play back AVID DNXHD video in Pro Tools output to AVID, AJA, or Blackmagic peripherals.

## Insert Bypass Shortcuts

Using a few key command shortcuts, you can now quickly enable/disable some or all plug-in inserts. These can be activated by insert row (A–E, F–J) or by type (EQ, Dynamics, Reverb, Delay, Modulation).

## New Automation Features

Power users have been asking for this for a long time; now Pro Tools 11 can write automation data in real-time during recording. Automation data will now be timestamped, so automation data will be preserved when moving clips.

## New Workspace Browser

A new 64-bit database engine enables ultrafast file searching. Now you can use a unified session and workspace browser to quickly locate your data files.

## Satellite Technology

Satellite mode, the ability to link multiple Pro Tools 11 systems, is now standard in HD11. Link up to 12 HD systems with a simple Ethernet connection. Is video playback slowing you down? Use a second computer to play video files using Video Satellite LE with Pro Tools 11. Video Satellite is now compatible with Media Composer 7.

## GUI Improvements

Along with improved display performance, AVID has refined the look and feel of the user interface.

## Session Import/Export

Now all Pro Tools users will be able to import and export OMF and AAF formatted files without having to purchase or install additional software. This is great news for Pro Tools operators who regularly exchange files with users of other DAW systems. There are advanced Import Session Data options, which were formerly only available with Pro Tools HDX systems. You now have the ability to bounce MP3 files to disk, which formerly required purchase of the MP3 Export option.

We will examine some of these new features in detail as we get into the various chapters in this book. There will be examples of how to maximize your system performance, activate and access your I/O, and make the most of the production techniques available with these new and expanded tools. It's good to know that all of your Pro Tools skills will now translate equally between the different levels of software. This is an amazingly versatile software platform; learning how to navigate through the program and use all of its features will make you a better engineer, and as a result, your music will sound better too.

# What Should You Bring to the Party?

In addition to having access to your own working Pro Tools rig, there are a few skills prerequisite to taking full advantage of the information presented to you in this book.

**Computers:** You must possess an above average understanding of computers in order to make the most of your Pro Tools software and, indeed, of any professional DAW software system.

**Engineering:** You should have a working knowledge of audio engineering concepts, signal flow, and gain structure, and have an understanding of the language of audio production.

**Music:** It helps to have a background in music. It may seem obvious to some folks, but there are terms and concepts in music production that we use constantly, and these terms are not always self-evident—such as *verse, chorus,* and *bridge;* or *tempo, crescendo,* and *intonation.* This is the language of music, and it's very handy for understanding and communicating ideas.

**Music Theory:** It also helps to have had some music theory education, even if self-taught. A good producer can tell if a particular note or chord is working within a song, and can make suggestions and fixes when it's not working. (This, of course, is subjective—never assume that a major 7th harmony interval is an accident.)

**Patience:** Pro Tools is a very deep and complex program, and it can take years to fully understand all the features. I've been using Pro Tools for over a decade, yet have learned many new things in the course of researching this book. I will give you basic information on each subject initially, then delve into deeper levels of understanding and complexity. Get familiar with the basics and practice your skills so you can move on to the more difficult material with confidence. First, learn the rules, after which you can choose which ones to break and when to break them. More on that subject later.

**Learn two ways to do everything:** This will come in handy in so many situations—such as when you are editing audio and need to cut out a clip and drag it to another track. I can think of at least four different ways to do it, each with its own set of advantages, each depending on the page I'm on and the editing tool I have currently selected. Be versatile and practice with the tools often; through repetition you will become an expert.

# How to Use This Book and the Related Online Materials

This book is designed to quickly bring you up to speed on the power and capabilities of mixing and mastering with Pro Tools, and to make you a more confident Pro Tools user overall. A good deal of this confidence will come from knowing that your system is properly installed and configured.

Some people are visual learners—that is, they need to see an image in order to get a firm grasp of abstract subjects. Throughout the book, you will see pictures or screen captures that illustrate the function or the process as described in the text. Use these to be sure you're viewing the same information or screen being covered on that page.

You will find a table of the keystrokes covered in each section of the book. All keystroke examples will be given in Mac user format. Here is a comparison table for basic Mac vs. Windows key equivalents to get started:

| Mac OS X | Windows 7 |
|----------|-----------|
| Control Key (Ctrl) | Control Key (Ctrl) |
| Option Key (Opt) | Start Key (Win) Also Called Windows Key |
| Command Key (⌘, Apple) | Alt |
| Return Key | Enter Key, Main Keyboard Only |
| Delete Key | Backspace Key |

There will also be a brief self-exam at the conclusion of each chapter so you can brush up on germane material before moving on. Experienced Pro Tools users will find this to be a particularly useful exercise, as some of the customary Pro Tools operations have been changed or modified.

I will give you as many practical uses and examples as possible so that you can benefit from shortcuts and a streamlined workflow. Work with these exercises as much as you can; it will make the techniques seem like second nature.

Since most of the mixing you'll be doing will be in stereo, we will assume that stereo is the default output or destination format for examples given in the book. I love mixing and mastering surround projects; I've won awards for surround TV mixing and have even chaired the GRAMMY® Surround Review Committee, but that's a topic for another book.

Feel free to do what I do when reading a book like this: dog-ear the pages, take notes in the margins, use a highlighter, paste a sticky note on important pages, keep it next to your DAW—whatever it takes to make this info easily accessible so that you'll actually *use* it.

## Video

We have prepared a number of videos showing in detail some of the operations discussed in this book. You can watch the videos any time just by selecting a video file from the online directory and double-clicking it. This requires the QuickTime plug-in for your Mac or PC.

## Session Data and Audio Files

We have included a number of Pro Tools sessions online so that you'll have access to the audio and session setups for each exercise as listed in the book. Just copy the session folders to the local hard drive you have already set up for Pro Tools sessions, and expand it into its own directory. You may want to create a new directory named "Demo Exercises" just to be sure this data is kept separate from your other sessions. As you create or open these sessions, select Save As in the file menu and name the session with your initials as the first characters of the file name. This way you can easily locate your version of the exercises and still be able to open the original files if you should lose some data or if you booger up the session beyond recognition.

In the event you are unable to read or import session data, you can import audio files into a new session by pressing Shift + Command + I and selecting the files to be imported. Using this method, you will have to import (or re-create) the other session settings, but the audio will be in sync if you align the start of each file to the start (or left-most end) of the sequence timeline in the Edit window.

## Additional Materials

We have dedicated a section of our website to provide you with easy access to downloads of handy and important files to aid you in your productions. These include pre-production planning worksheets, input lists, track sheets, mix cue sheets, a list of common Pro Tools error codes, and even a handy key command roadmap for those who easily tire of mousing every command.

## Updates

In some cases there will be information available online to supplement the material covered here. Occasionally some information will be updated to reflect new software releases or revisions. Check the Avid website from time to time to see what's new in the world of Pro Tools. You will also find a lot on their Support, Professional Services, and Training tab (www.avid.com/US/support ) that will help you in your pursuit of audio excellence.

# Chapter 1
# WHAT MAKES A GOOD MIX?

**M**ixing is the ultimate blending of multiple recorded tracks into a stereo (or multi-channel) master. This is accomplished by balancing the volume levels of recorded tracks in relation to one another in a pleasing fashion, panned between left and right speakers, resulting in a stereo "mix." Mixing is typically the final step in the recording process.

Musical preferences aside, one person's idea of a great-sounding mix does not necessarily translate to another's ears. This occurs for a variety of reasons, not least of which is the fact that while we all hear approximately the same frequencies, we do not all hear them the same way. The condition of your hearing depends on your age, your gender (believe it or not), and whether or not you've had prolonged exposure to excessive volume. Head injuries can also affect your hearing.

## Do Not Confuse a Good Mix with a "Good Song"

That song that makes you want to dance or pump your fists or sing at the top of your lungs is possibly eliciting those reactions for reasons very different than whether or not it was mixed well. While a great mix can certainly bring a smile to your face, it should make you want to listen harder to figure out how the mixer got that sound. Part of your job as a mix engineer will be to figure out what makes a mix sound good to you. Easy, right? One way to do this is to identify songs you like that are well balanced, use the full frequency spectrum, and sound good on a variety of speakers, sound systems, and headphones.

Another way to identify a good mix is to ask other engineers what they consider to be a well-mixed song or record. There are many interviews available online featuring great mix engineers talking about the songs they use for reference when preparing to mix. A story is told that at one point mixer Tom Lord-Alge used to listen to Def Leppard's "Pour Some Sugar on Me" every day before his sessions. Yes, I've tried it, but personally, I like to start with Donald Fagen's "Nightfly" or just about anything from Peter Gabriel and work forward from there. It also depends on the genre of music you're mixing; Ray Charles's "Genius Loves Company" is a textbook example of mixing lush string arrangements and great vocalists.

If you follow the steps outlined in this book, you will learn to make your mixes sound as good as they possibly can. The better your mixes, the better the chances that people will like your music, which begets more opportunities to make music, and so on.

## A Great Song vs. a Great Mix

Keep in mind what it takes to make a great song. According to gazillion-selling producer Keith Olsen, a great song consists of the following (in this order):

- A great composition
- A great performance
- A great recording

## What Makes a Bad Mix?

Oy, this is even more subjective and potentially contentious than deciding what makes a good mix. Here are some indicators of a bad mix:

- You can't hear one or more of the instruments or voices adequately.
- The fidelity is poor—frequency response is diminished, tracks are out of phase, there is audible unintended distortion, tracks are noisy, or any of a host of technical problems are present and audible.
- The mix does not translate—i.e., a song sounds okay on headphones, for example, but sounds awful on your stereo system.
- Phase problems—if the vocals disappear when you listen in mono, you have a phase problem.
- Lack of dynamic range—it is common these days to over-compress at the mixing or mastering stage; this can result in music that is loud but lifeless with little or no variation in dynamics. (See also "Level Wars" and "Metallica").

Once you establish your personal definition of a good mix, it will be much easier to draw a distinction.

## Think Like a Mixer vs. a Tracking Engineer

Most engineers will tell you that they listen differently during a tracking session than they do during a mixing session. For example, while tracking, you are attempting to capture a faithful representation of the actual sound of an instrument or voice while listening for sonic defects such as signal distortion or clipping, phase problems, and unwanted contact with microphones. This in addition to making sure musicians are playing/singing in tune and in rhythm. This behavior yields a good, clean recording that will be much easier to edit and mix. A mixer will certainly listen for those defects (because they have to fix them), but will also be listening for how instruments fit together sonically—e.g., how the bass and the kick drum frequencies either conflict with or complement each other. Some mixers are given the freedom to edit parts to thin out or clarify arrangements. In some cases, a mix engineer will bring additional parts into the mix to supplement existing instrumentation or to give the music a different feel. This is the creative part of the gig, and is potentially the most artistically and financially rewarding.

## Basic Mixing Tools

You have essentially three types of effects or tools to use when mixing in Pro Tools in order to achieve the optimal balance between tracks:

- Volume-based effects
- Time-based effects
- Spatial effects

## Volume-Based Tools

These include loudness control (or level), EQ (frequency equalization), and dynamics control (compression/expansion, gating). Typical use would be turning the volume of a part or track up or down to change the balance of that track as compared with other tracks in the mix. As an example, if the snare drum is too soft in a mix, you can increase the volume level +3 dB to improve the balance, potentially resulting in a more energetic-sounding mix. Likewise, adjusting a snare drum EQ by setting up a shelf EQ for +3 dB at 10 kHz may have a similar but subtler result. Compression is used to control the dynamic range of an instrument to allow it to appear at a more consistent volume level in comparison to other tracks in a mix.

## Time-Based Tools

Time-based tools include delay and reverb, pitch change and auto-pitch correction, and modulation effects such as chorusing or flanging. These types of effects are generally thought of as sweetening-type effects, as they change the character of a sound by adding ambience or sustain, as in the case of reverb and medium-long delays (> 50 ms). Flanging and chorus effects are created by means of introducing a very short delay (< 20 ms) and varying the period of the delay to produce a comb-filter-like sweep of the frequency spectrum, resulting in a whooshing or doubling sound.

## Spatial Effects

These include panning, stereo synthesis, and other manipulations of the stereo image. You can use simple effects to create a mix that takes full advantage of the space between the left and right speakers.

Panning refers to the panorama (or wide view) between stereo speakers. Pro Tools has the ability to pan signals by degree, from 100 percent left, to 0 percent (center), to 100 percent right.

Hard-panned stereo delays can be set to deliver repeats at different intervals per side, or to create a ping-pong effect, bouncing from speaker to speaker.

Stereo synthesis (or pseudo-stereo) uses comb filtering to divide a mono signal into frequency bands, which are then panned alternately to give a realistic impression of stereo while maintaining mono coherency.

Haas Effect: The human ear localizes the first sound it hears, even if the delayed sound is louder than the primary sound. So, if sound X originates from the left speaker, and is also reproduced from the right speaker but with up to 35 ms delay, your ears will still perceive the sound as having come from the left speaker. This is an interesting way to add some directionality and depth to your mix. Try it! Take a vocal track and duplicate it, panning one track hard left (< 100) and the other track hard right (100 >). Set the Pro Tools Nudge command to 10 ms and nudge one track later by 10, then 20, then 30 ms. The vocal track immediately appears to come from the left speaker at 10 ms, gets slightly wider at 20 and 30 ms, then becomes a slap delay at 40 ms. Probably not a technique you would use on every mix, but it can work wonders with a mono guitar track.

## Analog vs. Digital Workflow

Working in the analog world means using outboard gear or recording consoles to employ the aforementioned tools. In the DAW world, you have the advantage of using plug-ins (software components) to enhance or add functionality to your Pro Tools rig. If you use an interface that allows you to use outboard send/return effects in your system, you can still crank up your favorite piece of outboard gear and use it as a hardware insert on a track. For most folks, the complement of plug-ins that ship with Pro Tools will be more than enough to fulfill your desire for knob-twiddling.

### Creative Language vs. Technical Language

Engineers live in a world torn between two powerful forces—on the one side there is a room full of highly technical electronic equipment that requires a deep understanding of the scientific principles involved in working with sound. On the other side is the artist, passionately invested in exercising his or her creative vision. In the middle sits the engineer, whose job consists entirely of making the artist's music sound the best it can possibly sound. The tech side uses a lot of jargon and esoteric terminology to communicate ideas; the other uses emotional words and subjective language to communicate that which is unspeakable. Thelonious Monk is often credited with saying that "talking about music is like dancing about architecture." In other words, it's hard to describe with words something that has an abstract musical outcome. But as good mixing engineers, we need to try.

In teaching my classes, I ask students to describe the sounds they hear in emotional terms, then in technical terms. It never fails; students start out using descriptors such as "bright," "dark," "warm," "sparkly," or "ballsy." I have worked on just about every type of recording console under the sun, and I have yet to see one with a "sparkly" button or a "ballsy" knob. (Though I sometimes wish there was there was a "sucky" knob so I could turn it *down*.) Besides, that which means "sparkly" to me might really mean "screechy" to you. In order to really communicate effectively with one another, engineers have to learn to use more technical language that deals in Hertz, decibels, and milliseconds.

If a vocal track might sound too "dark" to you, try to put that into technical terms, like maybe it needs to be adjusted +3 dB at 10 kHz, or has too much energy below 250 Hz. Besides being good practice, this gives you the tools you need to communicate with other engineers in specific terms, and maybe even enables you to decipher what the guitar player means when he/she asks for that "brown sound." I guarantee you won't find a "brown" control on your EQ.

Practice listening to frequencies by range—can you identify low frequencies? Midrange? High frequencies? Even this gross distinction can help you figure out where to start looking for frequencies to adjust. Learn to discern a volume change of +/– 3 dB. This will enable you to make subtle changes in your mix. By the time you get to the 95 percent–done stage of your mix, you will be able to hear a change of half a decibel. That's when you know you're almost there.

Near the end of this book, you will find a chart displaying the basic frequency ranges of vocals and common instruments. Use this to help familiarize yourself with frequency ranges.

# Studio Basics: Control Room Environment/Acoustics

Your mixes will only sound as good as the room in which you mix. If you are working in a professional studio, or a project studio with an acoustically tuned control room, you will find that your mixes translate much better to other listening environments.

### Pro Studios

A professional studio will generally have a well-tuned control room, at least two pairs of monitor speakers, and a Pro Tools rig that is optimized and running the current version of Pro Tools software. Check out the studio before you book time, and have a chat with its staff engineers to get a sense of the room in which you'll be working. You may wish to bring your own plug-ins and iLok to ensure the availability of your favorite tools when it comes time to revise or update the mixes in another facility.

## Project Studios

A well-equipped project studio can have nearly the same capabilities as a Pro Studio but without the amenities of a full-time staff. This may prove to be more cost effective for your project in the long run, as long as the gear is up to date and well maintained. Again, check out the place before your session.

## Home Studios

Mixing on your own gear in your own room is perhaps the most cost-effective way to mix your project. Once you buy the gear, install it, and get it working properly, you can work any number of hours without blowing the budget. Plus, the commute home is easy-breezy.

Keep in mind, you have to be able to trust your mixes. If you are working at home in an 8'x 8'x 8' room plagued by resonance, standing waves, room modes, and comb filtering, you will likely have a tough time getting your mixes to sound good there—much less translate to any other playback system. There are too many facets of the topic of acoustics to delve into in this book, but there are many resources in other books and on the Interwebs to guide you through the process of setting up your control room for optimal acoustics. This is an investment that will pay many dividends over the life of your project and the course of your career.

You should take advantage of all the options when working on your project. It is not uncommon to record basic tracks in a professional studio, do overdubs in a home or project studio, edit at home, then go back to the Pro Studio and use its killer control room and giant Pro Tools rig for the mix. Use your resources wisely.

# Equipment

The question of equipping your home studio is really driven by the performance/budget equation. Since the quality of affordable recording gear has improved dramatically over the years, you can do essentially the same things on a laptop that it used to take a million dollars to do in a traditional studio. Sort of. You *still* need to understand how to use the tools.

**Step 1:** Figure out your budget. A thousand dollars is not too little; a million dollars is not too much. Pick a spot in the middle where you feel comfortable.

**Step 2:** Decide if you're going to be recording, recording and mixing, or recording/mixing/mastering. This will determine the tools you'll need to acquire.

**Step 3:** Do your research. Check the web, ask your engineer pals, talk to other people with home studios to see what they like. Test a lot of gear, if you can; determine what sounds good to your ears. Talk to your local pro audio salesperson to see what he or she suggests. If you're up front about your budget, he or she will help guide you to the right gear for your application.

**Step 4:** Write the big check.

**Step 5:** Take time to install everything correctly. Be patient and try not to book a session on the same day you get the boxes home. You'll be much happier with the results if you get it hooked up right the first time.

**Step 6:** Register all your software and check for updates. Ninety-nine percent of the time there's an update available for your software by the time you get it home from the store or it's delivered to your door.

**Step 7:** Save the boxes! You never know what you might have to ship back.

# Computers

## Mac vs. PC

Pro Tools runs rock solid on both Mac OS X and Windows 7 and 8, so it is now an equal-opportunity platform. (Whenever key commands are given in this text, they will be expressed in Mac terms.)

## Minimum Requirements

As of this writing, the Mac spec for running Pro Tools software is as follows:
- AVID qualified Apple computer with an Intel processor (http://avid.force.com/pkb/articles/en_US/compatibility/Pro-Tools-11-Qualified-Apple-Computers).
- Mountain Lion 10.8.5 and Mavericks 10.9 through 10.9.2.
- Total system RAM: 4 GB minimum, 8 GB required for video playback.
- See the AVID website for up-to-the-minute information (http://www.avid.com/US/support/find-support).

The PC spec for running Pro Tools software is as follows:
- AVID qualified Windows-based computer (http://avid.force.com/pkb/articles/en_US/compatibility/Pro-Tools-11-Qualified-Windows-Computers).
- Windows 8.1 Professional, Windows 8 Pro, Windows 7 Home Premium, Professional, or Ultimate edition with Windows 7 Service Pack 1 (all 64-bit).
- Total system RAM: 4 GB (8 GB or more is recommended).

See the Avid website for up-to-the-minute information (http://www.avid.com/US/support/find-support).

# Audio Hard Drives

Pro Tools is very particular about the type of hard drive used for audio recording and playback.
- Audio drive speed must be 7200 rpm or higher.
- Internal SATA audio drives are suitable for both Windows and Mac systems.
- You should *not* record audio on the system drive.
- eSATA drives are suitable for both Windows and Mac systems.
- External Firewire (1394) drives can *only* be used on Mac systems and should not be used in Windows systems.
- Firewire (FW) drive interfaces should use Oxford chipsets 911/912/924/934 in FW 400 or 800 configurations.
- Performance will be degraded if more than 4 FW devices are chained together on the same FW bus.
- Mixing FW 400 and 800 drives on the same bus may result in degraded performance.

## Work Drive vs. Backup Drive

The specs listed above are for your record/playback drives. You may use any system-compatible hard drive for your backups.

### Backup Plan

My motto: Only *save* if you want to keep the work you've done; only back up your hard drive if you want to keep the session you've just recorded/mixed/mastered.

In other words: *save* your session every chance you get, and *back up* your session drive *every day.*

Suggestion: Find an automated backup software solution that fits with your working style. In the IT world, data is not data unless it lives in three places.

### Hard Drive Lifespan Warning

Hard drives are not forever. Most drive manufacturers will warranty their drives for one to five years, depending on the manufacturer and type of drive. In reality, you may expect to get about three years of service from the typical drive, and then *only* if the drive is exercised (booted up) regularly.

### Long-Term Archival Planning

The Producers and Engineers Wing of the Recording Academy (aka the Grammy® people) have created an excellent document regarding archival and delivery specs for recording projects. This doc can be found at http://www.grammy.org/files/pages/DeliveryRecommendations.pdf

It's a lengthy read at 19 pages, but definitely worth the time invested if you plan to monetize your work in the future.

## Mixing Consoles

### Analog

Many engineers prefer to mix on an analog console using Pro Tools merely as a playback device. Level automation, EQ, dynamics, and other processing are done in real-time using outboard equipment.

### Digital

When mixing on a digital console, one can take advantage of total reset automation functions for ease in handling mix revisions. A digital console provides the option of using onboard EQ and dynamics processing (and the benefit of lower noise floor), or using outboard processing as needed.

## Outboard Hardware Processing

Using Pro Tools with outboard processing gear in a send/return configuration gives engineers the option of adding dedicated hardware bus compression (for example) while still taking advantage of powerful Pro Tools plug-in architecture and automation in order to perfect the sound of one's mix.

## Control Surfaces

There are two types of control surfaces available to Pro Tools users:
- Ethernet controllers such as the Euphonics Artist and Pro series, or the C|24 and ICON series consoles from AVID
- MIDI controllers from a variety of manufacturers

The advantage of Ethernet-based controllers over MIDI is the higher degree of functionality and processing speed of the Ethernet bus.

## Monitoring

It's best if you have at least two pairs of speakers to check your mix playback.

### Near-Field

This type of speaker is typically what you might find attached to the average home stereo (if there is such a thing anymore). Near-fields are fairly compact "bookshelf" speakers that are capable of delivering 85–95 dB with little distortion or coloration.

### Mid-Field

These are larger speakers that can deliver higher volume and broader frequency response. Mid-field speakers are great for checking the balance between the kick drum and bass guitar. Also, great for impressing the client.

Use an amplifier that matches the specification of each speaker you will be using (if applicable).

It is common to use powered monitors that are self-contained, meaning that they have built-in amplification and crossover electronics.

### Laptop

Since many people shop for and enjoy music on their laptop computers, you should occasionally check mixes on your laptop for reference.

### Automobile

I listen to most of my music in the car, so I tend to trust that sound system for checking mixes. You'll be able to judge pretty quickly what works and what doesn't just by cuing up mixes in the car.

With Pro Tools, you can even plug your laptop rig straight into your car stereo.

Just not while you're driving, please.

### Headphones

Another great way to check the fine details of your mix is to monitor on a good set of headphones. You'll be able to hear very distinctly many things you'd never pick out on speakers, such as noisy fades, talking in the background, squeaky kick drum pedals—all kinds of things. Don't mix exclusively on headphones, but *do* use them to check mixes.

### Earbuds

Man, I hate to admit it, but I spend a lot of time listening on earbuds—recreationally, not professionally. If I have to deliver MP3 mixes, I definitely check them on earbuds first.

## Listening Styles

- **Vary monitors:** Make sure you reference your mix on more than one set of speakers, particularly if you are unsure of your room acoustics.
- **Vary monitoring levels:** 85 dBC is a good reference level, but prolonged exposure can lead to hearing fatigue. Mix things up a bit, listen softly for one pass, louder for one pass. You'll be surprised at how much more information you can glean from this practice.
- **Listen from the hallway:** This has the same impact as turning the speakers down, but is a bit more "real world." I don't know anyone who sits directly in the parallax between two speakers all day long (except other engineers).
- **Take breaks:** Occasional breaks will lessen the chance of fatiguing your ears and give you a new perspective on your work.

## Format Information

Session data and format information should be determined before the mix begins, and your session created or saved using optimal format characteristics.

**Bit Depth:** Always mix to the highest bit depth available. Typically this will be 24-bits. Your noise floor and overall quality will improve dramatically, as will your plug-in performance.

**Sample Rate:** If the mix is destined for CD or web release, the format should be a multiple of 44.1 kHz (e.g., 44.1, 88.2 or 176.4 kHz). If the mix is destined for video or film, your sample rate should be a multiple of 48 kHz (e.g., 48, 96 or 192 kHz).When marketing people talk about "high definition audio," they are generally referring to a 24-bit 96 kHz recording format.

**File Format:** BWAV (Broadcast Wave, a flavor of the WAV file family). This is the preferred file format for most professional audio applications. If you are delivering a mix for inclusion in a video or a video game you may be asked to supply AIFF files. The difference is minimal; a BWAV file includes more metadata in the file header, such as information about the creation date/time. The audio data is essentially identical.

# Chapter 1 Review

1. What are the three effects types to use when mixing in Pro Tools?
    a. _____ effects
    b. _____ effects
    c. _____ effects
2. _____, _____, and _____ are examples of volume-based effects.
3. Reverb and delay are examples of _____ effects.
4. The Haas effect is an example of a _____ effect created with a _____.
5. Professional, project, and home studios are three types of _____.
6. Pro Studios can be expected to have at least two pairs of _____, an acoustically designed _____, and a Pro Tools _____.
7. Pro Tools will run on an Apple or PC computer with an _____ processor.
8. The Pro Tools 11 application can recognize _____ RAM.
9. It is recommended that Apple OS X computers running Pro Tools use _____hard drives, and Windows 7 computers should use _____ drives.
10. You should back up your session data to another medium at least once a _____.
11. Hard drives are designed to last about ___ years.
12. You can connect _____ and _____ controllers to Pro Tools for use as a control surface.
13. _____ -field speakers most closely resemble the sound of speakers from a typical home stereo system.
14. You should listen to your mixes on ____ sets of speakers, _____, and your _____system.
15. ___ dBC is a good reference level for mixing music.
16. Listening _____ is a physical by-product of the mixing process.
17. A mixing session should use _____ -bit resolution.
18. _____ kHz is a good sample rate for mixing music destined for CD duplication.

# Chapter 2
# THE PRO TOOLS SYSTEM

**W**ith the release of Pro Tools 9 and above, AVID no longer maintains three separate versions (M-Powered, LE, and HD). There are two levels of performance, Pro Tools and Pro Tools HD. The capacity of your system will be determined by the software license you have purchased and the hardware you use with it.

## Software Overview

Even the basic version of Pro Tools incorporates some of the features and functionality of Pro Tools HD:
- Automatic delay compensation is one of the biggest benefits of moving up to Pro Tools. The latest release of Pro Tools now offers ADC in both Native and HDX modes, which allows you much more flexibility in selecting and applying plug-ins, and saves tons of time in having to manually calculate latency.
- Use *any* ASIO or Core Audio compliant audio interface, using the Aggregate I/O (MAC only).
- I/O settings have changed; busses now include output busses as well as internal mix busses. Output busses can overlap, facilitating sharing of physical outputs. I/O settings can be imported or ignored on opening a session.
- DigiBase search and catalog functions have been enhanced.
- Import and export OMF/AAF sequences.
- Various time code and synchronization features have been added.

## Hardware Overview: Two Modes

Pro Tools provides a single software solution for all supported AVID hardware and third-party audio interfaces that utilize compatible Core Audio and/or ASIO drivers. If you're a long-time user of Pro Tools, this will be a revolutionary change in the right direction.

With your iLok attached, Pro Tools will run your session without *any* hardware interface attached.

Your Pro Tools performance will be determined by the authorization you have installed on your iLok device.

## 1. Pro Tools

- This is the standard software mode for Pro Tools when a non-HD audio engine is selected.
- Requires a Pro Tools iLok authorization.

### Features

- Up to 32 channels of I/O
- Up to 96 audio tracks (depending on sample rate)
- 128 instrument tracks
- 512 MIDI tracks
- 128 aux tracks
- 256 busses
- One video track

### Hardware Requirements

- Can be used with any supported AVID interface on Mac or PC. (Pro Tools version 9 and above does *not* support the 001 family or the first generation Mbox.)
- See the website for revised listings (http://avid.force.com/pkb/articles/en_US/compatibility/Pro-Tools-11-Approved-Audio-Interfaces-and-Peripherals).
- Any ASIO or Core Audio supported I/O should be recognized by the system.
- A number of audio interface manufacturers are now touting their Pro Tools compatibility, including Apogee, MOTU, Presonus and others. Check your local Pro shop or consult the Interwebs for more info.
- See the section on Aggregate I/O for more info on how to access your interface(s) within Pro Tools.

### Connection

Depending on your audio interface, any USB or FW port on the computer itself should work like a charm. Ports attached to USB keyboards typically do not have enough current to power hard drives or interfaces.

### Calibration

Each manufacturer has its own calibration or setup protocol, depending on which I/O you choose.

See the later section on system calibration for more details on DIY calibration methods.

### Plug-ins

Pro Tools comes with an extensive bundle of plug-ins and virtual instruments designed to get you up and running right away.

See the website for details: www.avid.com/US/products/Pro-Tools-Software/Specifications.

## 2. Pro Tools HD

- Pro Tools runs in this mode when you connect supported HDX or HD Native hardware and have selected the appropriate interface in your audio engine settings.
- Requires a valid Pro Tools HD iLok authorization.

## Features

As of this writing, the Mac spec for running Pro Tools software is as follows:

- Up to 192 channels of I/O.
- Up to 768 audio tracks (depending on sample rate).
- 256 instrument tracks.
- 512 MIDI tracks.
- 512 aux tracks.
- 256 busses.
- 64 video tracks.
- HDX systems take on the heavy lifting part of DSP using dedicated 64-bit floating point mix bus.

## Hardware

- Use either Pro Tools HD Native or Pro Tools HD interfaces. HD also requires HDX PCIe DSP Acceleration cards. HD Native also requires either a PCIe Core card or an HD Native Thunderbolt interface.
- An HD Native Core card gives you up to 64 I/O channels and 256 audio tracks using host processing (no DSP).
- HD Native can be used with the HD OMNI, HD I/O, and HD MADI interfaces.
- Each HDX card offers 256 voices and can support up to four HD series audio interfaces.

## Connection

- A multi-pair cable connects the PCIe card to the outboard audio interface(s).
- If you plan to use a computer, such as a Mac Mini or laptop that does not support PCIe cards, you will need an expansion chassis, PCIe controller card, and a cable to connect to the PCIe controller card in your computer. (The expansion chassis includes card and cable.)

## Calibration

The HD I/O audio interfaces offer access to rear panel calibration pots. See the later section on calibration for details.

## Plug-ins

Pro Tools HD runs the AAX 64-bit plug-in format. See the AVID website for more info.

# Outboard Gear

The really cool part about working with Pro Tools is the ability of the system to calculate and compensate for delays introduced by using outboard signal processing devices in a send/return configuration. In other words, you can take analog audio from any interface, send it to an outboard compressor (for example), return the compressed audio to the interface, and let Pro Tools calculate the round-trip delay. You can then set the system to compensate for that delay systemwide. Amazing.

Refer to the section on hardware inserts for instructions on how to connect your outboard gear.

## iLok

Pro Tools copy protection authorizations reside on an iLok USB dongle, which comes with your Pro Tools software. Most plug-in manufacturers now authorize their software via iLok as well.

The pluses: portable, safe, convenient, reliable. A great way to store all of your authorizations in one place and easily transport them from studio to studio or machine to machine.

The minuses: an iLok is small and can be lost or broken if you're not careful. Replacing authorizations can be very costly, unless you buy Zero Downtime (ZDT) license protection—a service that provides immediate access to your licenses in case your iLok is lost, broken, or stolen.

# System Calibration

To be certain your hardware and software are passing audio properly, you should devise a regular regimen for calibrating your system.

The basic principle is to apply a fixed input signal at a hardware input, then adjust each gain stage in the system to maintain optimal operating level. This level is typically 0 dBVU.

Some audio I/O hardware, such as the Avid HD|I/O, may have physical input calibration access via trim pots. See the owner's manual for exact calibration instructions for your interface.

### Optimizing the Pro Tools Environment

Tweaking Pro Tools for mixing is a little different than for recording and overdubbing. Once you have all of your parts recorded and edited, you will need to change some of the system settings to fine-tune your computer for the mixing and mastering process. It's fairly simple, and you can use this section as a guide to walk you through the steps in getting the most out your Pro Tools rig.

### System Usage Window

Having this window open on your desktop will keep you informed as to the performance of your Pro Tools session by displaying system status in real-time. On non-HD systems, you will see three meters in the Activity window:

**CPU:** Shows current computer CPU usage as a percentage of the allocated processing capacity.

**Disk:** Displays the amount of activity on the disk bus or busses as a percentage of total capacity.

**Memory:** Shows how much RAM is being used by Pro Tools.

## For HD|HDX Systems

The System Usage window displays the CPU, disk use, and memory as above, but you will see a few other windows as well, depending on the cards installed on your system.

**Disk Cache:** Shows the percentage of the allocated memory being used to cache audio in the session.

**Voices:** Shows how many voices of your total voice allocation are being used.

**Time Slots:** Shows how many time slots of your total allocation are being used.

## Playback Engine

Whether you are using Pro Tools or Pro Tools HD software, you will need to adjust the parameters for host-based operation. This is referred to as Optimizing Host-Based Pro Tools Performance. HD Native and standard Pro Tools users rely on host-based processing for recording, playback, mixing, and real-time effects processing. Even if you are using HDX DSP cards, the computer host still handles the chore of real-time effects processing.

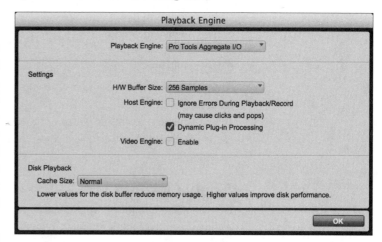

First, access the Playback Engine menu by choosing Setup > Playback Engine.

Your current engine will be displayed in the drop-down menu at the top of the Playback Engine window.

This menu will display a list of available connected I/O devices. Select your preferred device from the list. If you are selecting Pro Tools Aggregate I/O or any hardware other than the current device, Pro Tools will ask you to quit and restart in order to make that device active.

## Buffer Settings

When mixing, you should use the maximum buffer settings. This will allow you to use more effects to do more audio processing, particularly if you are using a large number of plug-ins. Locate the H/W Buffer Size menu, then select the highest setting available for your system.

High Hardware Buffer Size settings will result in an increase in monitoring latency and plug-in latency. However, latency is not an issue when mixing, because you won't have live musicians trying to play in sync with existing tracks.

## Host Processors

This check-box option asks if you would like to ignore errors during playback or record. The next statement says it all: "May cause clicks and pops." Ignore this command entirely and leave the box unchecked, unless you are having issues with record or playback errors. Should you decide to check it, you'll get an additional check box that, if checked, says it will "Minimize Additional I/O Latency." Again, this is not recommended, unless you are having record or playback errors.

### Delay Compensation Engine

This setting is no longer a part of the Playback Engine settings. If turned on, ADC will automatically be set to the highest delay limit (16,838 samples). Select Options > Delay Compensation to toggle the on/off state.

### Dynamic Plug-in Processing

This check-box option, if checked, will allow Pro Tools to only use CPU power on plug-ins when they are actually processing audio. Therefore, if they aren't doing anything, no additional system power will be used. This can be very handy if you have a large number of plug-ins in your session.

### Cache Size

This relates to Elastic Audio processing, and the RAM that AAE allocates for pre-buffering audio.

The standard setting is Normal, though you may need to raise the cache size if you encounter Elastic Audio errors, or lower it to free up memory for other system performance requirements.

### Apply Changes

When you have made all applicable changes to your Playback Engine, click OK to exit. Again, if you have made changes to your Hardware I/O Engine, you will have to quit and restart Pro Tools.

### Very Important Note!

If you start Pro Tools without the previously selected Hardware I/O connected and powered up, Pro Tools *will not* launch! Instead, it will go partway through the boot process, then pause to display an error message that reads "Pro Tools could not initiate the current playback device. Please make sure that the device has been configured correctly."

Don't freak out, just click OK, then relaunch Pro Tools while holding down the "N" key. This will bring up the Playback Engine dialog, which will allow you to select another interface or use the computer's built-in I/O. Click OK, and you're off and running. In fact, if you like, you can use that Hardware I/O modifier key command to call up the Playback Engine dialog every time you launch Pro Tools.

### Hardware Settings

The Pro Tools Hardware Setup menu gives you the option to set word clock source, sample rate, and digital I/O for your hardware, depending on the type of audio interface you have connected to your computer.

Any device that is supported by Core Audio drivers (Mac) or ASIO drivers (PC) can be configured in this menu, including your computer's built-in sound options via Pro Tools Aggregate I/O.

Choose Setup > Hardware to access the Hardware Setup window.

### Peripherals

This window identifies the connected I/O device, or allows you to select the device to be configured if you have multiple I/O devices connected.

## Sample Rate

If no session is open, you can use this window to select the default sample rate for Pro Tools operation. This would apply to new sessions as you create them.

Note: You can also specify a sample rate in the dialog window when creating a new session.

When opening an existing session, Pro Tools assumes the sample rate at which that session was created, in which case, the Sample Rate option will not be available for modification.

## Clock Source

This drop-down menu lets you select the digital clock source Pro Tools will use as a reference.

- **Internal:** Select Internal if recording analog audio, unless you have an external clock source connected.
- **S/PDIF (RCA):** This setting is for use when recording from the S/PDIF RCA digital input, and will synchronize Pro Tools to the output of the external digital device.
- **Optical:** Use this setting when recording from an optical digital source. You will have to select Format from the following menu in order to match the source signal.

## Optical Format

- **ADAT:** Choose this setting from the drop-down menu if your source is emitting ADAT optical digital multichannel output (Lightpipe) connected via fiber-optic cable. Supports session sample rates up to 48 kHz only.
- **S/PDIF:** This refers to optical 2-channel S/PDIF digital signal input via optical TOSLINK cable only.

## Launch Setup App

Use this command when setting up your third-party I/O device. This will launch the control panel specifically designed for your audio interface.

## Disk Allocation

This menu refers to the location of the folder from which your audio will be played back—per track.

Suggestion: if your session is displaying audio waveforms and playing back audio adequately, *do not change these settings.*

## I/O Settings

Choose Setup > I/O to access the I/O settings for your specific audio interface. From this window, you can select the following:

**Input:** Here you can name any input channel—per input, per device. You may also turn any input on/off, change routing, or add new input paths to your configuration.

**Output:** This menu is where you name output channels, activate or deactivate output paths, change routing, or add new output paths. You may assign an *Audition Path* for Audio Suite previews, Clip List auditions, and so forth. You may also assign a destination for the solo bus, if you choose to send it somewhere other than the main outputs.

**Bus:** There are major changes in bus assignments in Pro Tools. Whereas you used to see all available busses in this tab, now you only need to see the ones you create for your session. In fact, that's a good place to start. Let's set up a sample bus page for mixing in the box:

**Step 1:** Open the I/O > Bus tab and delete all bus paths. Yes, you read correctly, *delete all bus paths*. Now you can create a new, clean routing page with only the info you need for your session.

**Step 2:** Click on the New Path button. In the pop-up dialog, create 1 new Stereo path, name it "Monitor Out," then click OK. The new path will appear in the bus window.

**Step 3:** Tick the box next to the Mapping to Output window. This will create a link between the Monitor Output path you created and the I/O Hardware Output pair A 1–2. The Monitor Output bus will now become the main output assignment for all of the tracks in your session.

**Step 4:** You can create new busses in this window, or you can use the "new track . . ." command from the Send pane of the Edit or Mix windows to create a new Aux Input path as required for your session. Find that menu by clicking on the Send button, then click "new track . . ."

**Step 5:** To make a reverb send, create a Stereo Aux Input, sample based, and name it "Reverb"; tick the box marked "Create next to current track"; then click Create. In one simple operation, you have created a reverb send/return path with all assignments ready-made.

Repeat these steps as necessary to create new destinations for your session.

Note: This send/return operation is also described in the "Send" section of this book.

# Handy Pro Tools Functions

There are a number of Edit modes and Edit tools for manipulating sequence elements in Pro Tools:

## Edit Modes

### Shuffle (F1)

Shuffle mode allows you to move clips without leaving gaps, or to insert new clips between adjacent clips while forcing subsequent clips downstream. Also known as a *ripple edit*.

Trimming a clip in shuffle mode will affect the timing of all clips downstream.

Does not apply to MIDI notes.

### Slip (F2)

As the name suggests, this mode allows you to move or "slip" clips in time or between tracks.

Slip is the default mode for editing operations.

### Spot (F3)

Clicking on a clip in Spot mode brings up a dialog box that enables you to type in a precise time code or bar/beat location point. This is particularly handy if you've accidentally moved a clip from its original recording time and need to get it back to where it once belonged.

### Grid (F4)

Allows you to snap clips and MIDI notes to precise time increments, whether minutes/seconds, feet/frames, or bars/beats.

Moving a note or clip using Absolute Grid snaps the start exactly to the nearest time increment on the grid, even if it was initially between beats or other grid markings.

Relative Grid aligns the note or clip to the grid relative to its initial starting position. For example, if a selected clip is between beats 1 and 2 of the bar, it can be moved left or right in quarter-note grid increments, but will retain its original timing between beats.

## Edit Tools

### Zoomer Tool
The Zoomer tool zooms in and out on the timeline.

In Normal Zoom mode, the Zoomer tool remains selected even after the zooming.

Single Zoom mode allows you to use zoom once; the tool then reverts to its previously selected non-zooming tool.

### Trim Tool
Shortens or extends the duration of a clip or MIDI note by clicking and dragging the start or end of the clip.

### Selector Tool
Selects an area within a clip or track for editing or playback.

### Grabber Tool
The Grabber tool enables you to select an entire clip and move it within the track or to other tracks within the timeline.

### Scrubber Tool
Click and drag the Scrubber tool across audio tracks in the Edit window to locate an edit point or to hear a particular section within an audio clip.

### Pencil Tool
- Used for redrawing waveforms to eliminate a click or pop in an audio file. Must be zoomed in to the sample view level in order to activate.
- May be used for drawing in MIDI notes.
- May also be used for drawing automation breakpoints.
- Can draw various shapes for automating pan, volume, and other parameters. Shapes include line, triangle, square, random, and freehand.

### Smart Tool
Click on this gem to have immediate access to the Selector, Grabber, and Trim tools, depending on where the cursor hovers over a track, clip, or automation lane.

The Smart tool also performs single-click fades and cross-fades.

### Modifier Keys
The modifier keys are the Shift, Control, Option, and Command keys. (On a PC, those keys are Shift, Control, Windows, and Alt.) Pro Tools allows you to modify keystrokes and mouse-clicks depending on the modifier key. In some cases, various combinations of modifier keys will be used to achieve different results. For example, while Command + Click (Alt + Click on PC) brings up a tool menu for the cursor, Control + Command + Click (Control + Alt + Click in Windows) performs a variety of functions depending on the menu clicked.

See a list of topic-specific key commands at the end of each chapter.

### These Are a Few of My Favorite Tools

I leave the cursor tools set on Smart Tools all the time, except when I need a job-specific tool, such as TC/E or Pencil tool. Of the three choices for tools, I use the Trim tool, the Selector tool, and the Separation Grabber. These allow me to trim the beginning and end of a clip, highlight an area within a clip, and move clips or notes. The addition of the Separation Grabber allows me to highlight areas for deletion, copying, or moving without disturbing the original clip or having to change to another tool.

You can easily change editing tools by pressing Command + Click and selecting from the pop-up menu, or by toggling through options by using function keys F5–F10.

## Pro Tools Conventions

In order to navigate properly and find the functions we will be exploring, you should understand a few of the terms we will be using to describe the screen landscape and layout in the Pro Tools environment.

- **Window:** Refers to a main display component, such as the Edit or Mix window, or a plug-in window.
- **Pane:** Refers to a subset of an open window. An example would be the Tracks pane of the Edit window.
- **Button:** This would be any clickable graphic button that enables/disables functions or gives you access to a sub-menu. Clicking on the OK or Create button at the bottom of a pop-up window, for example.
- **Drop-down Menu:** Any menu that opens to display more options when clicked is referred to as a drop-down menu. The Window menu at the top of the Pro Tools menu bar is a drop-down menu.
- **Pop-up Window/Menu:** This could be a menu of functions or a new window that opens to display controls. Clicking on an assigned insert or send button displays a pop-up window.
- **Dialog Box:** Refers to any box that requires text input: naming a track, send, session name, or bounce file.

## Key Commands

Most of the common operations in Pro Tools can be activated by a mouse-click or a keystroke. If you have a two-button mouse, there is a whole world of shortcuts available to you by performing a right-click on a menu or pane. There are literally 30 pages of key command shortcuts in Pro Tools. Far too many to list here, but I will include the most used commands as they pertain to each topic of the book. Memorizing these commands will save you lots of time and many miles of mousing.

There are custom keyboards, keyboard overlays, and stickers available from AVID and other third-party suppliers. If you work in Pro Tools a lot, it may be worth your while to look into those options.

## Keyboard Focus

The Pro Tools Keyboard Focus determines how the alpha keys function on your keyboard. There are three modes of operation, which will allow you to directly select clips in the clip list, enable or disable groups in the group list, or perform an edit or playback command. Only one Keyboard Focus mode can be active at a time—which disables the other two temporarily. Here are the different modes:

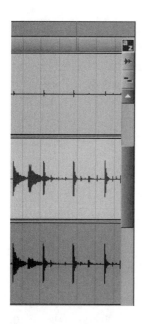

## Commands Keyboard Focus

Selected in the upper-right corner of the Tracks pane of the Edit window (see the a-z button), this enables a wide variety of single-key editing and playback commands accessible from the Edit window.

Note: Even if Commands Keyboard Focus mode is disabled, you can still access the command by using Control + the usual key.

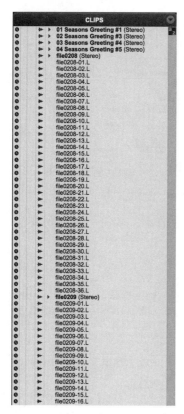

## Clip List Keyboard Focus

Selected in the upper-right corner of the Clips pane.

When enabled, you will be able to select audio and MIDI clips by typing the first few letters of the name.

### Group List Keyboard Focus

Selected in the upper-right corner of the Groups pane.

When enabled, you will be able to enable or disable groups by typing the Group ID letter that corresponds with the desired group.

### Keyboard Focus Access

Either click the a–z button in the panes as described, or type one of the following key commands:

| Operation | Mac | Windows |
|---|---|---|
| Command Keyboard Focus | Command + Option + 1 | Control + Alt + 1 |
| Clip Keyboard Focus | Command + Option + 2 | Control + Alt + 2 |
| Groups Keyboard Focus | Command + Option + 3 | Control + Alt + 3 |

# Summary of Key Commands

| Operation | Key Command |
|---|---|
| Cursor tool menu | Command + Click |

# Chapter 2 Review

1. With the introduction of _____, AVID no longer supports Pro Tools LE.
2. Automatic _____ compensation and third-party _____ support are now part of Pro Tools software.
3. Pro Tools requires the installation of a USB _____ in order to authorize the system for operation.
4. Pro Tools HD features near-zero latency record _____ with AVID _____ audio interfaces.
5. In order to run both native and _____ plug-ins, you will need to have an iLok authorized for Pro Tools HD, a set of _____ cards installed in your computer, and an AVID interface designed for _____ operation.
6. AVID HDX PCIe cards have dedicated _____ for processing.
7. The System _____ window tells you at a glance what percentage of _____ power you are using.
8. The Playback Engine dialog is used to fine-tune _____ performance.
9. _____ Hardware Buffer settings will result in greater latency, but are preferable during mixing to allocate more power to effects processing and _____ plug-ins.
10. Starting Pro Tools software holding the ___ key will bring up the Playback Engine dialog, enabling you to designate a specific device for audio ____.
11. The Hardware Settings > Clock Source menu lets you select the session clock reference, whether _____ or _____.
12. Pro Tools has two optical input settings, _____ and _____ Lightpipe.

13. You configure all input and output assignments using the _____ menu.
14. The four main edit modes in Pro Tools are _____, _____, _____, and _____ mode.
15. The main edit tools are the _____ tool, _____ tool, _____ tool, _____ tool, _____ tool, and the _____ tool.
16. The tool that performs multiple functions depending on the position within the track is called the _____ tool.
17. Pro Tools usually has several ways to complete an editing function. In addition to _____ commands, you can use numerous _____ shortcuts to complete tasks.

# Chapter 3

# MANAGING YOUR VIRTUAL STUDIO

It's a good idea to create your own sessions with custom settings that match your exact needs. These can be simple or complex, but it's worth your time to explore the options.

Session templates are a good place to start exploring Pro Tools capabilities and flexibility. Templates can help you understand how to create sessions and handle routing within Pro Tools. Open one of the music session templates to see examples of plug-in configuration, use of aux busses, and creation of a headphone mix.

Once you're familiar with these layouts, you can easily customize your own Pro Tools mixer to fit your mixing project.

You can even create your own templates to use in your next mix session.

## Configuring a Virtual Mixer in Pro Tools

I grew up on analog consoles; 16 x 4, 28 x 24, 64 x 8, 96 x 48, you name it. There were *always* limitations. Either there weren't enough inputs, or you had to sub-mix channels in order to get sufficient outputs, or there were not enough sends—you get the idea. One of the first reasons to fall in love with Pro Tools is the ability to create *exactly* the right console you need to work on each and every song. Since it's all virtual, you can grow or shrink the console anytime you want. Awesome feature.

### Tracks

Each recorded audio channel should have its own track, as should aux returns, sub-masters, MIDI tracks, and virtual instruments. This way you can balance and add effects to each element of a mix independently of the other audio tracks.

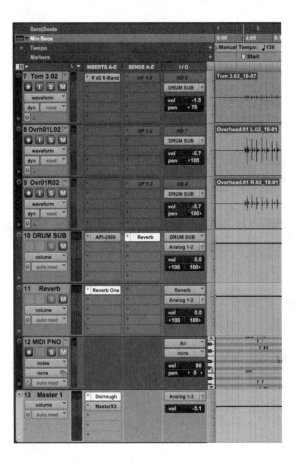

## Stereo Pan Depth

Pro Tools now lets you select the amount of attenuation applied to signals panned to the center in a stereo mix.

To access this setting from the Session Setup window, choose Setup > Session (Command + 2 on the numeric keypad). Select the Format tab, then click on the Pan Depth drop-down menu. You can choose from four different levels of attenuation:

- **−2.5 dB:** This is the only available setting for Pro Tools versions 8.x and below.
- **−3 dB:** This is the standard for many mixing consoles, and is the default setting for Pro Tools 8.1 and above.
- **−4.5 dB:** This is the standard center attenuation setting for SSL analog consoles.
- **−6 dB:** This is the standard for complete mono compatibility. Some US-made analog consoles offer the option of −3 dB or −6 dB center pan attenuation.

Changing these settings will result in a subtle change in the way sounds are perceived when panning across the center. A greater degree of pan attenuation will result in more subtle level changes as signal is panned from side to side. Experiment to see if your mixes translate differently using the various settings.

## Groups

You can combine tracks into *groups,* allowing you to control level, volume, pan, mute, solo, and editing functions of each member track with a single command.

Each group can have its own attributes or follow global edit commands. Grouped tracks maintain their own independent output assignments.

## Sub-Masters

Sub-masters differ from groups, in that tracks feeding sub-masters can retain their parameter control independent of a group. Tracks feeding a sub-master are summed together into an auxiliary bus, the output of which is fed to the main output Master Mix bus.

## Aux Sends/Returns

An *aux send* is a parallel output from a track or tracks, which can be used to feed a sub (as above) or provide input to an effect device/plug-in. An aux has a level control, which can send signal *pre-fader* (independent of track volume control) or *post-fader* (subject to track volume control).

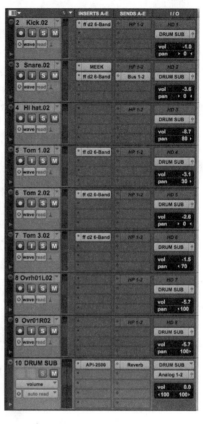

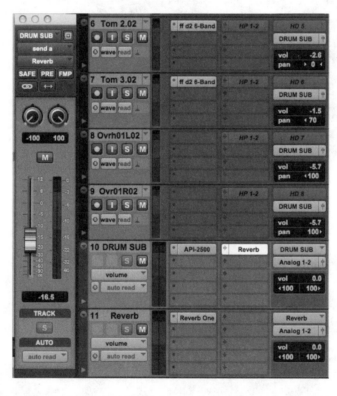

Pre-fader sends are used for headphone mixes, where you usually don't want the volume of individual tracks changing in the headphones while you adjust or solo tracks in your control room mix. Another use for a pre-fader send would be to maintain a constant level of effect send on a track regardless of the track volume.

Post-fader sends are used for reverb, delay, and other effect sends where you would like the send level to follow the track volume control. As an example, if you turn down the level of a vocal in a mix, you may want the reverb send level to get quieter in relation. You will find that your effects sound more balanced and natural when the send level scales up and down in relation to the track level.

## Inserts

Pro Tools gives you ten inserts per track in two banks of five each: A–E and F–J.

These can either be software plug-in inserts, hardware inserts, or instrument plug-ins.

With plug-ins and hardware inserts, the track signal is routed through your effect, then returned to the fader input on the same track.

Inserts are pre-fader on audio, auxilliary, and instrument tracks; inserts are post-fader on Master Faders.

You can bypass inserts by Command + Clicking on the Insert button on a track in the Edit and Mix windows, or by clicking the Bypass button on the plug-in window itself.

Repeat the command to toggle the in/out state.

Note: You can bypass the plug-ins in the A slot of every track by Option + Clicking on the Bypass button in any A slot plug-in window.

Likewise for plug-ins in the B slots, C slots, and so on. Repeat to toggle state.

Making an insert *inactive* will save system resources and voices. You can make an insert inactive by pressing Control + Command + Click on the Insert button. Repeat to toggle state.

Note: You can make all of the A slot plug-ins inactive by pressing Control + Option + Command + Click on an A slot Insert pane. (The Control + Option + Command key combination is also known as "the claw.") Repeat to toggle.

Right-clicking on a track insert button will being up a menu listing various insert options, such as Bypass, Make Inactive, Automation Safe, and a sub-menu for Automation Dialog.

## Insert Status Display

There are a number of display conditions indicating the current status of the insert:
- **Active, unmuted; plug-in window open:** The Insert button is white with black text.
- **Active, unmuted:** The Insert button is light gray with black text.
- **Active, muted; window open:** The Insert button is light blue with white text.
- **Active, muted:** The Insert button is blue with white text.
- **Clipped:** Regardless of mute state, text is red, plug-in meter shows red clip indicator.
- **Inactive:** The Insert button assumes track color, with black text in italics. When opened, the plug-in window will display the message "Plug-in Inactive."

## Clear Clip Indicator
To clear clip indicator, click on a red clip indicator, or press Option + C to clear all clips.

## Insert Order
Inserts process in series, so think carefully about the order in which you add your plug-ins. Every plug-in you introduce will have an effect on every other plug-in downstream. While there is no *best* way, there is a *common-sense* way to order your plug-ins. Let's have a look at the order for vocal processing, for example:
- **Insert A:** EQ 3 1-Band
- **Insert B:** Compressor/Limiter Dyn 3
- **Insert C:** EQ 3 7-Band

As always, your mileage may vary, but here's the reasoning behind this method:

- Filter unwanted frequency content *first*. That way your compressor doesn't have to respond to popped *p*'s or an overabundance of breath noise.
- Compress the vocal a moderate amount in order to control its place in the mix balance, dynamically speaking.
- Perform your EQ shaping after the dynamics have been tamed, and you will have a more consistent sound to work with. Plus, you won't accidentally be tripping the compressor with the +12 dB @ 16 kHz that you added to get the singer to sound breathy.

You will notice that there are no delay or reverb plug-ins added directly to the vocal track. Using time-based effects directly on a track makes it much harder to control the level of the track in the mix and to control the balance of effect to dry vocal as well. Instead, take a moment to create an aux bus to use delay and reverb as parallel-processed effects rather than series processed. You will have more control over the effect, and your vocals will sound much more distinct using this technique.

An additional benefit of using Pro Tools aux busses to administer effects is the obvious saving of CPU cycles. If you have 48 tracks of audio—each with its own reverb plug-in—you will be using much too much processing power to achieve your mixing goals. If one reverb isn't enough, create two, or four, or even ten aux busses to fulfill your reverb-drenched sonic fantasies. Better *10* than *48*. It's much easier to manage settings for a *few* reverbs than it is for a few *dozen*.

I hope this clarifies insert use and gives you solid techniques for maximizing your resources while striving for the best possible sound in your mixes.

## Insert Output Format
Plug-ins can be configured in mono or stereo, but remember that, because insert processing is done in series, inserting a stereo plug-in after a mono plug-in automatically makes all downstream inserts into stereo. You do not have the option of inserting a mono plug-in after a stereo plug-in.

There are three channel formats for plug-ins:
- mono-in /mono-out
- mono-in /stereo-out
- stereo-in /stereo-out

Note: Some plug-ins come in multi-mono versions rather than stereo or multichannel; they will behave as stereo devices in your insert chain.

## Moving Inserts
Simply drag the plug-in from the Insert pane on one track to the Insert pane on another track to move the inserted plug-in. All plug-in parameters will move along with the insert.

## Copying Inserts
Option + Drag the assigned insert to another Insert pane, whether on the same track or another. This is the fastest way to duplicate settings on an insert or plug-in.

## Deleting Inserts
Click on the Insert pane you wish to delete or clear. The first choice in the drop-down menu will be No Insert. Click on this command to delete the insert and its settings from that insert slot.

Note: You cannot undo this operation. Save your session before deleting anything you may wish to change your mind about.

## Using Hardware Inserts

If you have favorite pieces of signal processing equipment that you would like to use in the Pro Tools environment, you can use hardware inserts to connect your gear on individual tracks or sub-mixes.

You must use corresponding inputs and outputs on your I/O to send and receive using the hardware inserts. For example, if you are sending signal out of the Pro Tools hardware inserts on output channels 3 and 4, you must return the processed signal to input channels 3 and 4.

## Compensating for Delay in Hardware Inserts

Delay compensation can be applied to hardware inserts using the H/W Insert Delay page in I/O Setup. Here's how:

- Access the Setup menu and select I/O.
- Click on the H/W Insert Delay tab.
- Type the delay value (in milliseconds) into the input field where you have connected your hardware insert.

## Calculating Delay When Using Hardware Inserts

Check the user's manual for the device you are about to connect; there may be a processing delay value listed in the specs.

If not, you can use Pro Tools to determine your hardware delay. This is a bit of a process, but well worth the time invested. Follow these steps:

**Step 1:** Enable ADC.

**Step 2:** Set the Timeline Scale to measure minutes/seconds.

**Step 3:** Create two mono audio tracks.

**Step 4:** On the first track, create a short burst of tone using an oscillator plug-in. Alternately, use an audio file with an obvious visible beginning, such as a snare drum hit.

**Step 5:** Use a hardware insert on track 2.

**Step 6:** Bus the track 1 output to the input of track 2 and arm track 2 for recording.

**Step 7:** Record the test tone or other audio from track 1 onto track 2.

**Step 8:** Zoom in and measure the distance between the beginning of the audio on track 1 and the beginning of the audio on track 2 using your Cursor tool to highlight the clip.

The resulting difference is the round-trip delay time of your external processor. This is also the value you will enter into the H/W Insert Delay page.

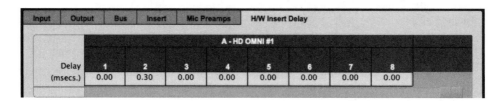

| Input | Output | Bus | Insert | Mic Preamps | | H/W Insert Delay | | | | | |
|---|---|---|---|---|---|---|---|---|---|---|---|
| | | | | | A - HD OMNI #1 | | | | | | |
| Delay (msecs.) | 1 | 2 | 3 | 4 | 5 | 6 | 7 | 8 | | | |
| | 0.00 | 0.30 | 0.00 | 0.00 | 0.00 | 0.00 | 0.00 | 0.00 | | | |

## Sends

- Pro Tools gives you ten sends per track in two banks of five each, A–E and F–J. These can be accessed from either the Edit or Mix window, or from the send's own pop-up window.
- Sends are available in mono, stereo, or multichannel on all audio tracks, auxiliary inputs, and instrument tracks.
- Pro Tools sends can be configured pre- or post-fader, much like an analog console.
- Sends are used for parallel processing; returns are audible in addition to the un-effected audio.
- Note: A send must return to the mixer via audio track, auxiliary input, or instrument track in order to be audible in Pro Tools.
- Send level, pan, and mute can be set to follow group assignments. In other words, if you change the send parameters for one member of a group, all members' sends will change in relation.

### Common Uses for Sends

- Sending audio to a real-time plug-in or hardware insert for processing, as in reverb or delay.
- Creating a separate simultaneous mix or sub-mix. Drum or vocal sub-mixes would be examples of sub-mixes you would use regularly.
- Creating one or more headphone mixes that are separate from the main monitor mix.
- Sending audio to a plug-in key input.

### Assigning a Send to a Track

- Enable Sends View in the Edit or Mix windows. For example, choose View > Edit Window Views > Inserts A–E.
- Click the Sends A–E pane of the track on which you would like to add the send. Select which output or bus destination you would like to send signal to.
- You may assign a send to a mono or stereo bus or output.
- Send level can be adjusted from the send level fader that pops up when you click on a send.

### Send View Options

- The default view for sends is by bank (A–E and F–J). The number of sends displayed is related to the height of the track being viewed.
- You can set your send view options to display one send at a time (instead of five at a time) with send meter and all send controls visible all the time. To display Send A in the track send column, choose View > Sends A–E > Send A. From this pane, you can choose to view other sends from the drop-down menu.

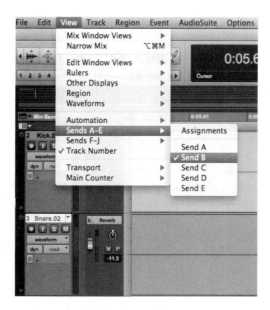

- To return to all-sends view, simply choose View > Sends A–E > Assignments or View > Sends F–J > Assignments.

## Send Status Display

There are a number of display conditions indicating the current status of the send:

- **Active, unmuted; window open:** The Send button is white with black text.
- **Active, unmuted:** The Send button is light gray with black text.
- **Active, muted; window open:** The Send button is light blue with white text.
- **Active, muted:** The Send button is dark blue with white text.

- **Inactive:** The Send button assumes track color, with black text in italics. When opened, all controls in the Send window will be grayed out.
- **Clipped:** Regardless of state, text is red; Send meter shows red Clip indicator.
  To clear clip indicator, click on a red clip indicator, or press Option + C to clear all clips.

### Opening Multiple Send Windows

Pro Tools normally allows you to have one Send window open at a time. It may be convenient for you to have more than one Send window open at once, in which case you can Shift + click on the Send button to open a Send window and keep it open on the desktop. Use the same technique to open more Send windows. You can also click the red Target button on open Send windows to keep them open.

To close these windows, click on the red Close button in the upper-left corner of the Send window.

### Create and Assign a New Track from a Send Pane

This is another very cool feature of Pro Tools. Using this feature, you can create and define a new send, create and define a new destination, and name the track, all in a single operation. Here's how to do it:

From any active track, click on a send and scroll down to the option named "new track . . ."

The New Track dialog window will pop up, offering you the option to select send width (from mono and stereo through 7.1), the type of destination (aux input, audio track, or instrument track), choose samples/ticks, and name the destination track as well.

If you click the button marked "Create next to current track," then click "Create," your new destination track will show up in the track list immediately below the track in which you selected the send.

This is a big time-saver over the old multi-step process, but know that you can still assign sends and create destinations in separate steps if you prefer.

## Master Faders

Whether or not you create a Master Fader on your virtual console, it *is* present, and the main output of your mix goes through it. Adding a Master Fader gives you a knob and the ability to make adjustments to the final gain stage output.

Note: Adding a Master Fader does not change the resolution of your mix, even on fades—if it's a 24-bit session it will remain a 24-bit mix all the way down to –infinity dB.

### Master Faders Do Not Use Excessive DSP Resources

A Master Fader track gives you an opportunity to meter your mix *post-fader* so you know whether or not you're clipping the mixer output.

### Creating a Master Fader for Stereo Master Volume Control

- Using the Create New Track dialog (Shift + Command + N), create a new stereo Master Fader using the pull-down menus.
- Set the output for each track to the main audio output path, usually outputs 1 and 2 of your main hardware interface.
- Set the output of the Master Fader to the main output path.

### Creating a Master Fader for Sub-Master Input Trim

- Using the Create New Track dialog (Shift + Command + N), create a new stereo Auxiliary Input track.
- Bus the output of the desired tracks to the input of the Auxiliary Input track.
- Create a stereo Master Fader; assign the output to the same bus that feeds the Aux In track.

### Inserting Plug-ins on the Master Fader

This is the same operation as inserting a send on a track. Click the Send window and select from the drop-down menu.

### Uses for a Master Fader

- Control and process Output mixes.
- Monitor/meter outputs, busses, or Hardware outputs.
- Control sub-mix levels.
- Control effects send levels.
- Control the level of bussed tracks (sub-masters).
- Apply Dither and other effects to entire mixes.

## Clearing Clipped Signal Indicators

- You can clear a signal clip indicator on a visible track meter by clicking the red clip indicator.
- Clear all clip indicators by pressing Option + C.

## Dither

- Whenever you convert from 24-bit to 16-bit audio, there is a likelihood of introducing digital distortion at very low volume levels. This distortion is not usually audible at normal signal levels, but can become audible on fade-outs, reverb tails, or in quiet passages.
- *Dither* is the process of adding low-level random noise to digital signal, essentially in the last bit. This serves to mitigate distortion, which is potentially more audible than the noise introduced. This has become a common practice when mixing for CD or another 16-bit audio destination format.
- Pro Tools comes with two dithering plug-ins for use on your Master Fader: Dither and POWr Dither.

### Noise Shaping

Noise shaping is part of bit reduction/dithering, and refers to the process of moving the resulting noise to a higher frequency range (above 4 kHz) where the human ear is less likely to detect it.

Maxim is a dynamic maximizer plug-in that features a noise shaping component, as well as parallel processing and dithering—a nice feature set for use during mixing or mastering.

## Turning up the HEAT—Harmonically Enhanced Algorithm Technology

This is a new analog emulation software add-on for Pro Tools HD users. Designed by Dave Hill (of Summit Audio and Crane Song fame), this software is activated across every channel of your mix to bring the sound of multi-channel analog audio processing to your DAW (for those of us who don't own a Neve console and can't afford a Fairchild compressor).

It's worth watching the video of Dave explaining the analog recording and mixing process to understand what this software does, but activating and playing with it in your mix is the best way to experience the effect.

The controls are very simple—two knobs: Drive and Tone. There is a Master Bypass button, as well as individual channel bypass buttons. The master section also has an on/off switch to free up DSP resources. A PRE button on each channel allows you to select pre- or post-insert processing.

### Drive Control

This relates to the amount of distortion derived from overdriving the circuits of an analog mixing console. In the default 12 o'clock position, there is no HEAT processing active. Turn the Drive knob to the *left* to add analog console emulation and even-order harmonics. Turn the knob to the *right* to add the sound of tape saturation and odd-order harmonics.

### Tone Control

Does what it says, pretty much. Turn the knob to the left to emphasize lower harmonics; turn the knob to the right to emphasize upper harmonics.

### HEAT Meter

The channel meters at the top of each channel strip display how much HEAT processing is being applied at that moment. The brighter the meter, the more effect being added. The Master HEAT meter displays the amount of process being applied to the entire mix.

### PRE Button

This places the HEAT process pre-inserts when lit, post-inserts when unlit. Experiment with pre/post positioning to hear how the final sound is influenced.

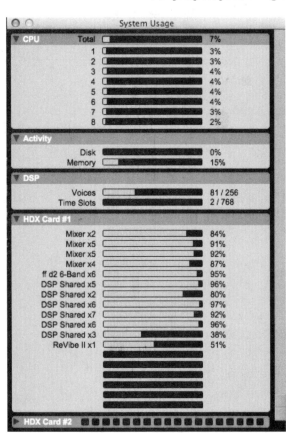

Note: HEAT can only be used on audio tracks. Aux busses and instrument tracks will need to be printed to audio files in order to process with HEAT.

Another note: HEAT uses a healthy amount of DSP, so you should be aware that you may run out of system resources much more quickly when using HEAT on your mix. Opening a session with insufficient DSP resources may result in HEAT being deactivated or in AAX plug-ins deactivated. (HEAT processing takes precedence over AAX plug-ins in the processing hierarchy.)

Tip: Keep your System Usage meters running during mixing to measure your use of system resources.

### Mixing with HEAT

Since the controls are deceptively simple, you may not be aware that the complex harmonic processing going on behind the scenes is impacted by subtle changes in frequency content, dynamics, overall amplitude, and the number of active channels being processed . . . kinda like a real console.

The best results will be achieved by getting your mix to sound the best it can sound *before* you add HEAT processing. Then activate HEAT and compare with the un-effected mix frequently to determine if the net results are in line with your vision for the mix.

Note: Be aware that adding HEAT to each song in your collection of mixes may result in a slightly different sound quality for each. As I mentioned previously, this is a very dynamic process, and it will respond differently to different program material.

There are no pre-sets to store or recall, but you can import HEAT switch settings via the Import Session Data command (Shift + Option + I). You will need to rely on your own ears to be sure you're using the appropriate amount of HEAT in each of your mixes.

After some experimentation, I felt that HEAT had a positive effect on some mixes and that I would definitely like to hear what HEAT sounded like in a mastering session where the focus was on subtlety and overarching tonal qualities.

### HEAT, According to Its Designer

I *loved* the results of using HEAT in my mixing tests but couldn't figure out a way to effectively convey to you how it does what it does. So I called Dave Hill, who developed this ingenious software.

In response, Dave asked, "How do you describe a color or distortion? HEAT works because you can't describe it—the more complex the function, the harder it is to describe. HEAT uses a complex algorithm to accomplish intensive calculations. But it only has two control knobs. It's an extremely complex thing made easy so that anyone can use it." He continued:

> HEAT started out four years ago at a NAMM show as a way to bring analog sounds into the digital recording process. It got complicated very quickly, because the analog recording chain introduces some weird processes, from the single-ended, even-order harmonic distortion of analog consoles to the hyped record/playback equalization curves of analog tape machines, and the +6 dB-per-octave rise in high frequencies associated with multitrack head gap.
>
> HEAT is written for TDM because it needs massive computing power in order to work across 48 tracks. TDM provides dedicated processing, and is expandable to accommodate higher track counts.

Dave's suggested starting place: activate HEAT right away, turn it up two clicks, *then* build your mix.

Personally, I found HEAT to affect mixes differently depending on the program material and how many tracks were active in the session. Hard to describe, but what a great *color* to bring to the mix.

## Organizing Your Tracks

There are a few schemes for laying out your tracks, mainly based on traditional music-production techniques developed for use with analog multitrack tape on analog mixing consoles.

A common method is to order your tracks in the Edit window from top to bottom, beginning with the drums, then bass, followed by chordal instruments (keys, guitars, etc.), vocals, and ending at the bottom with effects returns and finally the Master Fader. If you think of mixing in terms of "building a house," you will start with a foundation of drums, then work your way up through the frequency spectrum (and complexity of sound), and ending with the focal point of the song—the vocals. We will get in depth on this technique later in the book.

Another approach is lining up your tracks in the Mix window from left to right, beginning with drums, bass, chord instruments, vocals, and effects returns tracks. This emulates an analog console layout and places the vocal tracks closest to the center of the console. The theory is that you'll be spending more time mixing the vocal tracks, and keeping them in the center of the console also puts you consistently in the parallax of the speakers.

Your mileage may vary.

## Edit Window Layout

### Info Display

You can customize the information displayed in the Edit window by selecting from the drop-down menu at the top of the screen (View > Edit Window Views). From here you can choose which of the following to display:

- Comments
- Mic Preamps
- Instruments
- Inserts A–E
- Inserts F–J
- Sends A–E
- I/O
- Real-Time Properties
- Track Color

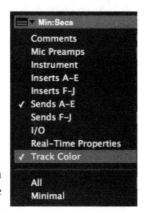

Note: These selections are also available from a drop-down menu located on the top left of the Edit window just below the Rulers display.

### Displaying Rulers

Depending on the time-base and editing style of choice, you can select the rulers best suited for your editing operation. You can also display Markers, Tempo, Meter, and other song-specific parameters in the Ruler display. To access these options, select the drop-down menu View > Rulers.

### Group Assignments

At the lower-left corner of the Mix window, you will find an area titled "Groups." The default setting includes just one group—All—which, when highlighted, ties all tracks together for editing commands. Cut, paste, copy, move—whatever commands you assign to the global group will affect all tracks. You can add up to 104 groups of tracks of your choosing by selecting the Name field for each track and typing Command + G, then naming the group. It will then be added to the list of groups and can be turned on or off by toggling the state within the Groups window.

You should create a new group for every instrument that occupies more than one track. In a typical rock band recording, you might have a group for each instrument, which will make mixing an easier task. For example:

- Drums
- Bass
- Guitars
- Keyboards
- Background Vocals (BGV)
- Main Vocal (VOX)

Having a group assignment for each species of tracks will make it much easier to balance levels between instruments, perform edits, and engage automation functions.

## View Tracks

The Tracks View pane lives on the left-hand side of the Edit window and shows/hides tracks in the Edit and Mix windows based on selection or type. There is a drop-down menu in the Tracks pane to allow access to these selections as well as sorting options.

The Tracks pane can be shown or hidden by accessing the drop-down menu View > Other Displays > Track List.

You can number the tracks in the Tracks pane as well, which is really handy for finding your way among a mix containing 96 tracks.

Select from the drop-down menu View > Track Number.

## Hiding Tracks

If you have chosen the View Tracks window on the left-hand side of the Edit window page, you now have the option to modify the number of tracks viewed in the Edit window at any time. Simply click the dot icon next to a track name to alternately hide or make it visible.

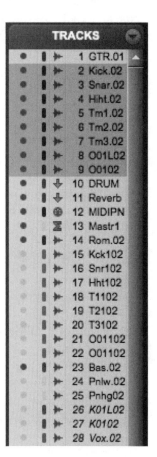

This is a handy function if you have a large number of tracks in your mix and want to concentrate on just a few of them. Or, if you have recorded alternate takes or solos and don't need the info in your Edit or Mix windows, you may remove them from view. Keep in mind, hidden tracks will still play and utilize output voices. If you truly want a track to be silent, you should mute all clips within the track, make the track inactive, or delete the track from the sequence. If you choose the latter method, be sure to make a copy of your session and rename it so you don't lose any track info permanently.

Note: Group commands still apply to hidden tracks, whether or not you can see them. Don't be surprised when that muted scratch vocal track makes a mysterious and unwanted reappearance after you un-mute a visible track in the same group. When in doubt, make a track inactive first, then hide it. For hiding multiple tracks, there is a Hide Inactive Tracks command within the Tracks column drop-down menu.

## Grid Settings

If your song was recorded to a click track, then it's super easy to have all of your editing commands conform to precise bar and beat lines. Find the Grid pane at the top of the Edit window and click the arrow. This allows you to access and modify grid settings.

Typically, you will resolve the grid to quarter notes when in Bar/Beat mode, though this will depend on the tempo of the song and complexity of the edit you are performing.

Set your Edit mode to Grid or Relative Grid so that everything you edit or move will snap to the beat.

If your song was not recorded with a click track, you can still use Grid mode, but it will not relate to the tempo of your song. In which case I would suggest setting the grid resolution to minutes/seconds and using it for elapsed time reference only. Use SLIP mode for editing, in this case.

You can guesstimate tempo using the TAP TEMPO mode in the Metronome pane of your Transport window by turning the Conductor track off, highlighting the BPM rate, then pressing the "T" key in time with the music.

## Nudge Settings

As in the description of Grid settings above, go to the Nudge settings pane in the Edit window and click the arrow. This gives you access to the nudge resolution.

Again, if you have recorded your song to a click, then using Bar/Beat mode in the Nudge settings window will allow you to move clips or notes in beats or fractions of a beat. This can be really handy for editing MIDI performances.

Whether recorded to a click track or not, I leave my Nudge mode set on minutes/seconds and use 10 ms as the base nudge resolution. I have found that adjusting timing on performance recorded as audio tracks requires much finer resolution and may only need to be moved 10 or 20 ms in order to rectify a late hit or a missed downbeat.

The following keys access nudge commands:
- The comma key (,) moves the selected clip or note 1 increment earlier.
- The period key (.) moves the selected clip or note 1 increment later.
- The "M" key (m) moves the selected clip or note 10 increments earlier.
- The forward slash key (/) moves the selected clip or note 10 increments later.

If your nudge resolution is set to 10 ms, then the comma (,) and period (.) keys move in 10 ms increments, and the "m" and "/" keys move in 100 ms increments.

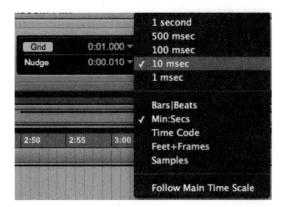

## Color Palette

Changing the color assignments on elements of your screen layout will help you quickly locate and identify tracks, clips, markers, or groups of tracks. Sometimes the vocals just look cooler in purple. Either way, the Color Palette gives you the option to organize by color.

Double-click in the color bar area left of the track name in the Edit window, also at the very top of the channel strip in the Mix window. (Or select Window > Color Palette). This will bring up the Color Palette window, which allows you to choose colors for tracks, clips, groups, and markers.

Note: If the Marker option is grayed out, you will need to go to the Preferences window, click on the Display tab, then click the Always Display Marker Colors button.

Select the track(s), clips, group, or marker you'd like to modify. The currently selected color will be indicated by a highlighted swatch in the Color Palette window. You can select a new color by clicking the desired color swatch.

The Undo command (Command + Z) gets you back to the previously selected color. You can also click the Default button in the Color Palette window to return to the factory setting for the selected item.

## Memory Locations/Markers

Memory Location markers are a great way to identify and navigate quickly to positions within your session. This will be a huge timesaver when working on specific sections of a song during mixdown.

Use markers to identify the beginning of a take, a section of a song, or an event within a song that you'll need to locate again easily. Markers are numbered sequentially as you add them.

To display the Markers ruler, select from the View menu: View > Rulers > Markers.

There are four ways to bring up the New Memory Location dialog. First, locate to the desired point in the timeline, or highlight a clip. Then do one of the following:

- Press the Enter key on the numeric keypad.
- Control + Click in the Markers ruler near the top of the Edit window.

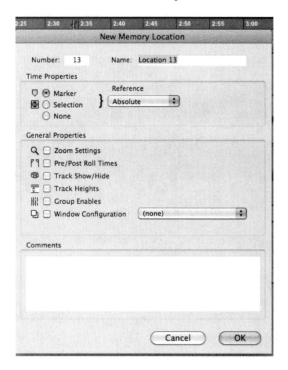

- In the Memory Location window, Command + Click.
- Click on the + sign in the Markers ruler.

- As you create a new marker, the New Memory Location window will reveal a number of options, including typing a Marker Name, changing the Marker Number, selecting Time Properties, and setting General Properties.
- Marker Memory Location relates to a particular point in the timeline.

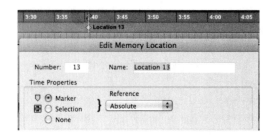

- Selection Memory Location relates to a user-designated Edit selection in the timeline.

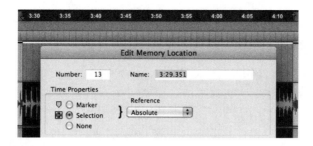

- Select or highlight a clip in the timeline.
- Create a Memory Location, then hit Enter to add marker.
- Click the Selection button, then click OK.
- The clip selection is stored along with the other Memory Location parameters.

General Properties Memory Location (the "None" button) relates to a number of session settings that can be stored and recalled.

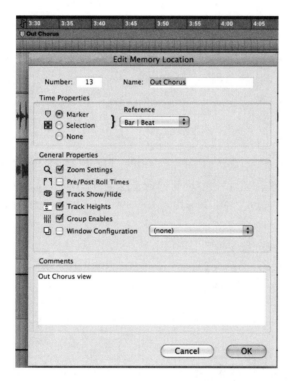

Storing or recalling General Properties data can include screen views, zoom settings, pre- and post-roll times, track show/hide status, track height, and enabled Edit/Mix groups. This does not necessarily require location information.

This can be handy when viewing the drum kit or vocals during editing, or for recalling your Master Fader metering layout during the mixdown process.

To store these details, set up the screen view to your satisfaction, then check the boxes corresponding to the information you wish to save.

See the section below on Window Configurations to set up specific window layouts and views, which can then be recalled in the General Properties pane.

Each session can store up to 999 Memory Locations.

These are stored and displayed in the Memory Location window accessed by typing Command + 5 on the main keyboard, or by accessing the Window > Memory Location window.

Memory Locations can be recalled, modified, created, and deleted from this window as well.

- Command + Click to add a new marker.
- Option + Click to delete a marker.
- You can sort, edit, and renumber markers in this window as well.

To locate a specific marker, type its number on the numeric keypad in this way: decimal point, (number), decimal point. Locating to Marker 2 looks like this: .2. You can also click on the Marker icon in the Marker ruler of the Edit window or in the Memory Location window. You will find a list of your markers in the Memory Location window.

Markers can be moved by grabbing the Marker icon in the Marker ruler and dragging it to the desired location.

Note: Markers will snap to Grid settings if moved while Grid mode is selected.

Common section marker names include:

- Intro
- Verse (or Verse 1, Verse 2, etc.)
- Chorus (or Chorus 1, Chorus 2, etc.)
- Solo
- Bridge
- Breakdown
- Modulation
- Outchorus
- Coda
- And any other section names that might apply to the piece you are working on

Note: I like to add a marker at the very beginning and the very end of the song as well; this helps to easily identify the length of the entire song when it comes time to bounce the mix to disk.

### To Delete a Marker

- In the Marker ruler, drag the Marker icon down until it turns into a Trash Can icon. When you release the Mouse button, the marker will be deleted.
- In the Memory Location window, Option + Click on a marker to delete it from the list.
- These operations can be undone (Command + Z).

## Window Configurations

This tool allows you to set up a screen view for each selected operation you wish to use, save it as a Window Configuration, and instantly recall the screen view.

Note: This is superhandy for getting a focused view of just the tracks you need to edit, such as drums or vocals, without having to reconfigure your screen manually for each operation.

### Here's an Overview

First, open the Window Configurations window by locating the drop-down menu Windows > Configurations > Window Configurations List, or pressing Command + Option + J.

Start by making a new Window Configurations setting named Default with your basic window layout of choice. You can add comments for your reference in the field provided. When you click OK, it will be saved to Position 1 in your Window Configurations list.

Use this as the main layout for editing or mixing.

Now let's make a new window layout featuring just the drum tracks, open the Clips, and open the Strip Silence window (Command + U).

Open the New Configuration menu from the main Windows menu (Window > Configurations > New Configuration . . . ) or from the drop-down menu in the Window Configurations window.

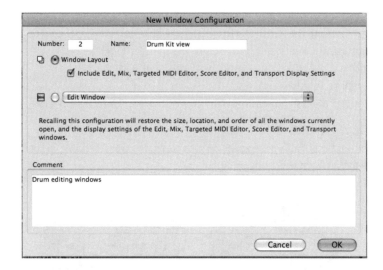

Select Window Layout and type the name "Drum Kit view" into the Name field. Press OK and this will be saved to Window Configuration 2.

Recall your Default Window Configuration by typing Period (.) 1 Asterisk (*), or .1*

This should recall your original default window layout.

Next, type .2*

This should restore your Drum Kit view layout.

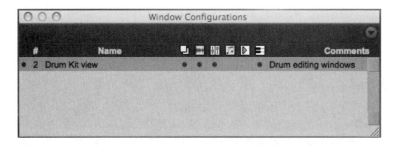

Note: If you have selected Auto-update Active Configuration from either drop-down menu, changes to the active view will be saved with the Window Configuration. The number of the currently selected Window Configuration will be displayed in parenthesis next to the Window menu at the top of the screen.

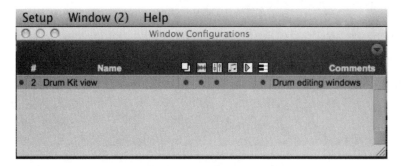

I suggest leaving this item unchecked unless you need to modify your view, or you may accidentally overwrite your configurations. There is no undo function for this operation.

To delete a Window Configuration, select the subject configuration from the Window Configuration page and choose Delete (name of configuration) from the drop-down menu. Another way to delete the setting is to Option + Click on the subject configuration in the Window Configuration menu. It will then be permanently deleted.

Your Window Configuration settings will be saved with your session.

You can import Window Configuration settings from other sessions using the Import Window Configurations command in the Import Session Data > Import Options dialog.

## Mix Window Layout

Many of the functions and views in the Mix window are also available in the Edit window and are accessible from the same menus.

 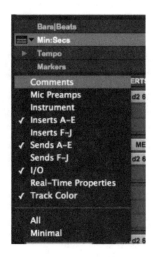

## Memory Locations

The Memory Locations window allows you to see all of the markers you've added to the session, edit the data stored in each, and view them in order of creation or numerical sequence.

## Window Configurations

This window allows you to create and store custom window views for instant recall. This can be super handy when editing and mixing, because you can instantly focus your attention (and screen real estate) on just the tracks you are editing and hide the remainder until you need them again.

These configurations can be stored as memory locations too, giving you nearly instant access to single or multiple track views.

# Transport Window

The Transport window shows basic transport controls (Return to zero [RTZ], Rewind, Fast Forward, Go to End [GTE], Stop, Play, and Record buttons), counters, and some MIDI controls.

It can also be configured to show Pre/Post roll, Count-off, Tempo and Metronome settings, as well as enabling the Tempo ruler (or Conductor track).

While these commands can always be accessed at the top of the Edit and Mix windows, the Transport window can be a floating window as well. This allows you to position it on your monitor screen wherever you may need it. The quick access key command is Command + 1 on the numeric keypad.

# Editing Operations

Okay, now that we have some of the mechanics squared away, let's get down to editing the tracks in preparation for mixing.

As we get into practical application of the tools and techniques presented here, you will quickly see that there are at least five different ways to do everything in Pro Tools. Or so it would seem. This is not designed to make you crazy, but rather to give you options at every turn. If you know at least three ways to solve a problem, you will naturally choose the method that is fastest or most efficient. With some practice, you will find that a lot of these operations become muscle memory as a result of having used them so often. Saving, for instance. You should save your work often, and the fastest way to do this by far is to use the keyboard to type Command + S. Most DAW users can find that command in the dark, and you should too. As I tell my students, only save if you like what you've done and want to keep it.

# Playlists

If you have recorded tracks with alternate playlists, you should review them to be sure you're using the master take.

View alternate playlists by clicking the Track View Selector button in the Edit window, then selecting Playlists. This will open a Playlist lane beneath each track showing you all takes for each track.

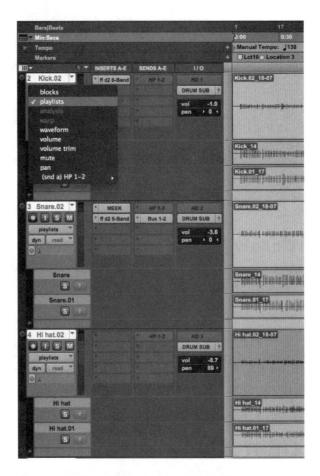

You can also view a playlist by clicking the Track Name button and selecting the number of the playlist you wish to view.

Note: Playlist views subscribe to group assignments, so if you switch playlists on a Drums group member, for example, the view of all Member tracks will switch as well.

By activating All in the Groups pane, all tracks will switch their playlist views when one is changed.

## Duplicating Tracks

You can duplicate tracks by selecting Track > Duplicate . . . (or Shift + Option + D), then completing the instructions and clicking OK.

Note: You cannot undo this operation. You will have to delete the track manually if you want it gone.

To delete a track: Highlight the track name to be deleted; select Track > Delete . . . A pop-up window will then ask you if you're sure, because there are active clips within the track. Click OK to delete. You cannot undo this operation either.

## Cleaning Tracks

Whether you recorded every instrument yourself or inherited tracks from other engineers, you will find it necessary to edit portions of the tracks if you find them to be noisy or otherwise unusable. Pro Tools gives you a number of ways to deal with the job of cleanup.

## Strip Silence

Pro Tools has a handy function called Strip Silence that eliminates sections of a clip falling below a user-defined threshold level.

If you select a clip and open Strip Silence (Command + U), you will see a dialog box giving you access to four adjustable parameters allowing you to define "silence."

As you adjust the Strip Threshold, you will see the clip view divided up into smaller and more numerous sub-clips. Use this to determine the minimum amplitude at which a new clip will be created.

The other parameters—Minimum Strip Duration, Clip Start Pad, and Clip End Pad—allow you to force durations onto the new clips to be created. In other words, you can set a minimum duration, or extend each clip end by 100 ms, or add a few ms of silence before the clip start time.

This is a great way to remove noise between tom hits, headphone leakage between vocal lines, or amp hum between guitar lines.

Click the Strip command button to complete the operation once your selections have been fine-tuned.

Note: You can always undo this operation later in the process by selecting all the stripped clips and pressing Command + H to heal the track, thereby restoring it to its original state before the Strip Silence operation was performed (as you long as you didn't move the sub-clips or change the timing).

## Noise Gates

Another way to mute noisy tracks is to use a Noise Gate plug-in on the offending track.
- Noise gates can be set to reduce or completely silence the track volume when the signal level falls below the gate threshold.
- Gate attack, release, and duration can be set to your specification in real-time, tailoring the ADSR of the gating function.
- Frequency-dependent gates allow you to focus in on the part of the spectrum where, say, a snare drum has the most energy, and use that specific part of the frequency spectrum to open the snare gate—regardless of how hard the drummer is whacking the floor tom.
- Gates are super handy for drums, horns, noisy amplifiers, audience mics, and so forth.
- They can be "keyed" or triggered by audio from another track, providing the option to have the kick drum control the opening of the gate on a bass guitar, for example.
- Gates can also be used to trigger a reverb send or return for heightened dramatic effect, opening when the vocalist sings above a particular volume level.
  The more you mess with gates, the more applications you will discover.

## Manual Editing

There will be times when using Strip Silence or a noise gate just doesn't give you the control you need to clean up your tracks.

An example would be cleaning tom tom tracks on the recording of a drum kit.

There's usually too much going on in a drum kit to use Strip Silence, since the background noise on tom tracks typically doesn't drop low enough to consistently differentiate a tom hit from a snare hit.

A noise gate would suffer from the same false triggering issues and is not smart enough to respond to an overlapping cymbal crash with a natural decay time.

The solution is to clean your tracks manually using Pro Tools editing functions to separate and mute unwanted clips.

Once you have isolated a tom hit, separate the clip (B). Next, highlight the clip before the tom hit and cut (X), delete (Delete), or mute it (Command + M). Do this operation for every tom hit on the track(s).

Now you can fine-tune the duration of each tom-hit clip and fade in or out as the context of the performance dictates—i.e., if tom hit 1 occurs without any cymbal bleed, you can draw a 500 ms fade after the waveform dissipates, and it will sound pretty natural in the mix. If there is a cymbal crash concurrently with a tom hit, you may need to extend the end of the tom hit clip by two seconds, then draw a two-second fadeout.

Do this with every tom hit on all tom tracks, and you should have a cleaner-sounding drum kit overall, as the toms usually contribute noise and tonal coloration that take away from the sonic quality of the drum kit.

## Mute Clip vs. Cut and Remove

Okay, so you've decided to invest the time in editing your tracks manually. Do you delete the unwanted clips or do you simply mute them? I do either or both, depending on the situation.

If there is nothing but noise, hiss, or hum in the space between actual playing or singing, I will delete the unwanted bits. Likewise, if the track is silent for most of a take, I will truncate the clip(s) to include audible parts only.

If there is any performance to be edited—for content or for mistakes—I like to mute the track. This grays out the clip but allows me to see if there are still waveforms present, and gives me the option to easily bring those clips back into the mix if I want them. Especially useful if I've edited a tom track and lost a subtle fill.

## Consolidating Clips

Once you have cleaned your tracks and made your final edits, you should consolidate a heavily edited track into a new contiguous clip by using the Consolidate command from the Edit menu at the top of the page.

This serves to make a single file out of many edited clips, thereby conserving CPU and disk load.

It also makes it much easier to keep track of files when it comes time to back up your session.

Note: While consolidating a clip does write a new file to disk, that file does not contain any of the underlying automation information, nor any of the plug-in or insert processing.

# Summary of Key Commands

| Operation | Key Command |
|---|---|
| Session Setup Menu | Command + 2 (Numeric Keypad) |
| Bypass Insert | Command + Click - Insert Button |
| Bypass All "A" inserts | Option + Click – "A" Insert Button (or B, C, etc.) |
| Make Insert Inactive | Control + Command + Click – Insert Button |
| Make All "A" Inserts Inactive | Control + Option + Command + Click – "A" Insert Button |
| Clear Clip Indicator | Option + C |
| Copy Insert | Option + Drag to New Insert Slot |
| Keep Send window open | Shift + Click – Send button |
| Create New Track | Shift + Command + N |
| Import Session Data | Shift + Option + I |
| Import Audio | Shift + Command + I |
| Add Group | Select Tracks, then Command + G |
| Undo | Command + Z |
| New Memory Location | Enter (Numeric Keypad), Control + Click – Marker ruler, Command + Click – Memory Locations window |
| Memory Location Window | Command + 5 (main keyboard) |
| Delete Memory Location | Option + Click - Marker |
| Go To Memory Location | .Number. (e.g., .2. for Marker 2) on the Numeric Keypad |
| Window Configurations | Command + Option + J |
| Strip Silence | Command + U |
| Transport | Command + 1 (Numeric Keypad) |
| Save | Command + S |
| Duplicate Track | Shift + Option + D |
| Heal Separation | Command + H |
| Separate Clip | B, or Command + E |
| Cut | X, or Command + X |
| Copy | C, or Command + C |
| Paste | V, or Command + V |
| Mute Clip | Command + M |
| Nudge Left | , (Comma) |
| Nudge Right | . (Period) |
| Nudge Left x10 | M |
| Nudge Right x10 | / (Forward Slash) |

# Chapter 3 Review

1. Pro Tools now offers four levels of pan depth for varying degrees of stereo image accuracy when panning across the center position. These are _____, _____, _____, and _____.

2. An Aux send is used to send parallel _____ from a track to a bus for _____ to effects or outputs.

3. ____-fader sends are used for headphone mixes, while _____ sends are used for effects sends.

4. Pro Tools allows you to use either software _____ or hardware inserts on each track. A hardware insert requires physical inputs and outputs on your audio _____ in order to connect _____ hardware.

5. Hardware inserts use additional _____ allocation.

6. Inserts appear in order, creating a chain of _____ processing.

7. _____ plug-ins are usually added to Aux Inputs, and _____ are routed from the tracks to the reverb plug-in. This saves processing horsepower.

8. Copying an insert or a send from one track to another is easily accomplished by using the _____ + _____ command to copy the insert or send with all settings intact.

9. Calculating hardware _____ in Pro Tools involves recording a small piece of audio through a _____ send/return path and comparing it with an undelayed sample.

10. Pro Tools gives you ____ sends and ____ inserts per track.

11. Creating a _____ gives you a control with which to vary the output level of your mix.

12. The process of _____ was developed to reduce the amount of digital noise associated with bit reduction from 24- to 22-, 20-, or 16-bits.

13. Noise Shaping refers to the process of moving _____ to a less audible frequency range.

14. HEAT is analog circuit emulation software for use with Pro Tools _____ systems.

15. Among the information displayed in the Edit and Mix windows are:
    a. _____
    b. _____
    c. _____
    d. _____
    e. _____

16. You can display several rulers at the top of the sequence window, including markers, _____, and _____.

17. Hiding tracks from within the Tracks window will remove them from the _____ and _____ windows, but they will still be audible as long as they are active.

18. You can create very accurate edits using the Grid and Nudge settings. The nudge key commands are ____, ____, ____, ____ and they usually correspond to –10x, –1x, +1x, and +10x the Nudge settings.

19. Use the _____ key on the numeric keypad to create a new marker. Each session can store up to _____ memory markers.

20. You can save your session by typing the key command _____ + ___.

# Chapter 4

# MIXING TOOLS

I n this section we will look closely at ways to manipulate your recorded tracks, whether bouncing processed audio clips to disk or using real-time plug-ins.

## Audio Suite Plug-ins

When used with clips selected in the sequence timeline, Audio Suite plug-ins create (or *bounce*) new files with plug-in settings. These new files replace the original clips in your timeline.

Audio Suite processing saves real-time processing power by permanently printing your effects and is accessed via the main Audio Suite menu.

Saving the session with the effects already printed gets you one step closer to having the session prepped for long-term archival or delivery.

## Working with Plug-in Inserts

### AAX—Avid Audio eXtension (Native)

- These plug-ins employ host-based processing to effect signal in real-time during playback.
- AVIDRack Plug-Ins: These are the 70+ free plug-ins that ship with Pro Tools software. Check the AVID website for the latest list of plug-ins shipping with Pro Tools.
- Most of the virtual instruments used in Pro Tools use AAX Native technology.
- Because Pro Tools is now a 64-bit application, its architecture is much more efficient. This means you can now access more virtual instrument plug-ins in real-time than you ever could before, as the application is no longer limited to just 2 GB of physical RAM.

## AAX—Avid Audio eXtension (DSP)

- This type of plug-in requires the proprietary AVID PCIe cards, which use dedicated Digital Signal Processing (DSP) chips for real-time signal processing power, as opposed to using the host computer.
- The HDX system provides the power necessary to record/overdub/playback with minimal latency. (Not to be confused with ADC, which merely compensates for system latency on playback by making everything . . . later.)
- This is the most powerful type of Pro Tools system, and requires a tower computer to accommodate the DSP cards.

Note: You can only run AAX plug-ins on your system if you have the HDX processing cards. You can run AAX plug-ins on any system, but you need the HDX hardware to run both types.

## Inserting a Plug-in on Your Track

- Pro Tools gives you 10 plug-in slots per track.
- You are limited only by your computer's processing power and RAM allocation.
- If you are working in the Edit window, click on the triangle icon in the Insert window. This will bring up an alphabetized list of all the plug-ins you have installed on your system. Mouse over a category—EQ, for example. The list will expand to show all available EQ plug-ins by name. Mouse over and select one of the EQ plug-ins and click. This will insert that plug-in on your track in the Insert slot that you selected.
- To insert multiple plug-ins, select sequential slots and repeat the above procedure.
- The inserted plug-in will open in your main window as a floating pop-up window. You can position this window anywhere on your screen, preferably someplace where it won't interfere with the other windows. Clicking on the plug-in name will close the plug-in window.
- If you click on the name of another plug-in, the previous plug-in window will close, and the newly selected plug-in window will open.

## To View Multiple Plug-in Windows

If the plug-in window is already open, click the red, square Target button to keep that particular window open. Then a new window will open for the next plug-in you select. You can leave any number of plug-in windows open while you work. Likewise, if you Shift + Click on the plug-in name in the insert window, that plug-in will open and stay open until you close it manually.

Note: If you are working on a Pro Tools HDX system, Pro Tools software will let you assign AAX plug-ins in any order. This is new for Pro Tools. You should be aware that inserting an AAX plug-in between DSP plug-ins will use additional voices. This will only be an issue if you are working on a massive mixing session with many tracks, and may result in track muting if the total number of available voices is exceeded.

## Plug-in Manipulation

Turning them on/off: Some plug-ins use a proprietary on/off button; most do not.
Bypass vs. Make Inactive:
- Bypass turns off the effect of the plug-in.
- It still uses system resources.
- Inactive plug-ins retain their settings but do not use system resources.

Plug-ins use a series of mouse-adjustable controls to modify the various parameters displayed onscreen, which can be then be compared A/B style to default settings. Once you find a setting you like, the parameters can be saved for later recall by accessing the

Plug-in Settings menu in the Plug-in window. This menu lets you copy, paste, save, and import settings, as well as establishing the destination for storing plug-in settings.

## Copying Plug-in Settings

If you really dig the EQ sound you got on your Left Overhead track and want to duplicate that on the Right Overhead track, you have a few options for matching settings.

Copy/paste settings: In the plug-in window for the left overhead, locate the Preset menu, then select Copy Settings (Shift + Command + C). Insert the same plug-in on the Right Overhead track, locate the Preset menu, and select Paste Settings (Shift + Command + V).

Save the setting. If you found a sound you think you may use again and again, you can save it for easy future access. In the Left Overhead plug-in window, locate the Preset menu, then select Save Settings As . . . This gives you the option to name the setting and save it among the other pre-sets for future use.

Option + drag. This may be the quickest way to duplicate a plug-in; just copy the entire plug-in with settings intact to the destination insert. (Option + drag). Voila!

## The Secret of the Right Mouse-Click

The right mouse-click gives you access to hidden menu options depending on where you click. For example, right-click on the track name to show a menu of track options.

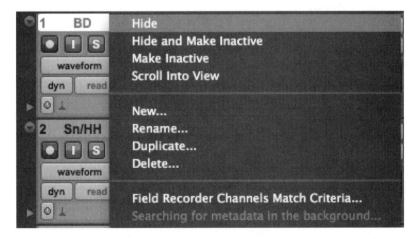

Right click on a plug-in name in the insert pane to show a menu of plug-in options.

This is a handy shortcut in case you forget the secret keystroke combination.

### Printing Tracks with Real-Time Plug-in Effects

If you're working on mixing a project that you may need to revisit in the future, you should consider printing your tracks with effects.

Note: This is particularly valuable if there's chance that the project will be opened on a system without the same plug-ins or on a different DAW platform.

This process differs from printing files using Audio Suite plug-ins, in that the process is done in real-time using aux tracks and internal bus routing. Here is a standard method for bouncing individual or group tracks:

**Step 1:** Create a new mono or stereo Aux Input track. Click on the Output pane of the guitar source track and select "New Track . . ." Name the aux track some variation of the source name—e.g., Guitar SUBMIX.

**Step 2:** Select the bus named Guitar SUBMIX for the output destination of the track(s) you wish to print with effects.

**Step 3:** Create a new mono or stereo audio track (Shift + Command + N) and name it Guitar Bounce.

**Step 4:** Select Guitar SUBMIX as the input for the Guitar Bounce track. Click the Record-enable button, and record a clip from the beginning of the song. This new clip will be named Guitar Bounce_01, and assuming you have engaged ADC, it will be perfectly in sync with the other tracks.

**Step 5:** Deactivate the original source tracks for this bounce so that they no longer play back or use system resources.

The newly created Guitar Bounce track now contains the guitar clips you bounced with effects and will be the track you use while mixing.

The process will be the same whether you bounce one track or several, as long as you remember to route all of the source tracks to the Aux Input you create.

### Side-Chain Effects

- Kick and bass compression: Tighten up the low end of your mix by using a kick drum–keyed compressor side chain input on your bass track to decrease the volume of the bass when the kick drum hits.
- Kick drum augmentation using an oscillator: Use the kick drum to key a noise gate open/close on an oscillator track generating a 20 Hz tone.
- De-essing: A de-esser controls the volume of a narrow frequency band using a combination of EQ and compression. See instructions on building a de-esser later in this chapter.
- Note that side-chain processing with AAX plug-ins uses additional voices.

# Processing Tools for Your Toolkit

There are loads of tools available for you to create pristine, raw, or downright crushed and mutilated mixes. These tools generally fall into one of four categories:
- Frequency tools
- Dynamic Range Control tools
- Pitch tools
- Time-Based tools

# Frequency Tools

## EQ

**Equalization (EQ):** Provides you with the means to increase or decrease the amplitude of a particular band of frequencies.

**Parametric EQ:** Gives you the ability to select a frequency center point, vary the bandwidth (or Q) of the effected frequencies, and make them louder or softer. Multi-band parametrics can be very powerful tools when combined to make notch filters.

**Quasi-Parametric EQ:** Pretty much like the parametric, but without the Q control. Used on many mid- and lower-priced mixing consoles.

**Graphic EQ:** Separates the frequency spectrum into fixed bands (typically 31), each with its own level control, which can then be made louder or softer independent of adjacent frequencies.

**British Style EQ:** Made popular on British recording consoles, consisting of four equalization bands:
- High Shelf
- Upper mid-band parametric
- Lower mid-band parametric
- Low shelf

EQs also include notch filters, bandpass filters, high-pass filters, and low-pass filters.

Pro Tools ships with three basic EQ plug-ins that are quite flexible, giving you the option of using a single band or up to seven bands of EQ that are user configurable. Think of the 7-band as a super-British EQ.

AVIDRack EQ 3 plug-ins:
- 1-band equalizer, with 6 curve and filter profiles
- 4-band equalizer, each band fully parametric.
- Low frequency, lower-mid band, higher-mid band, high-frequency bands.
- 7-band equalizer, adds a mid-frequency band and 2 dedicated filters

## Using EQ to Fix Problems

You may encounter a problem that can only be fixed by applying the right EQ. As an example, I once mixed a string quartet project in which the cello had a very *pronounced* low G note, which became even more prominent when trying to balance the string section. Everything else was fine: good tone, no buzzing or wacky noises. The solution came in the editing stage before mixing, where we tried a number of solutions to cure the loud notes. In the end, we doubled up two parametric EQ bands set to reduce amplitude by –16 dB each at the same center frequency, essentially creating a very narrow notch filter, which reduced the amplitude –32 dB at exactly 98 Hz. The mix was automated to bypass the EQ circuit *except* for when the offending G note was played. The result was amazing! The entire performance was in balance, sounded full, and no change in tone was discernible.

Yes, I could have used a) a limiter set on *crush*, or b) a narrow band boost EQ keying a limiter to achieve the same effect (essentially, constructing a low-frequency version of a de-esser), but I wanted to accomplish this without using compression, due to the ballistics of a compressor and its inability to recover quickly after such dramatic gain reduction.

## Using EQ to Enhance Sound

EQ can be used to emphasize frequencies that are not sufficiently present in a recording, such as the high end of cymbals or the low end of a kick drum.

There are two ways to apply EQ:

**Subtractive EQ:** Making a selected frequency (or frequencies) quieter.

For example, kick drum: subtracting –3 dB @ 400 Hz, medium Q, with a parametric equalizer can make a kick drum fit better with a bass or guitar track.

**Additive EQ:** Making a selected frequency (or frequencies) louder.

For example, electric guitar: adding +3 dB @ 3 kHz with a peak EQ can make an electric guitar sound more dominant in a mix.

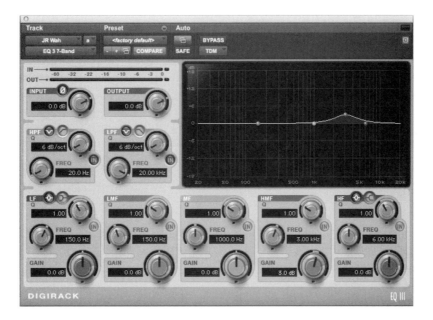

Make subtractive EQ changes before you start adding gain to your mix. Folks generally tend to reach for additive EQ right away—I strongly suggest you determine what your objective is first, then see which frequencies you can reduce in order to achieve the objective. (See the kick drum/bass guitar example.)

Note: A well-recorded instrument may sound great alone, but might not work with other instruments in a mix. For example, an acoustic guitar recording might sound full and have a wide frequency response but compete with other instruments in a mix. It may be necessary to thin out some of the low-end response of the acoustic guitar by reducing the low frequency shelf EQ by –3 dB at 150 Hz. The resulting sound may not be the perfect solo acoustic guitar sound, but it will work better in context with other chordal instruments.

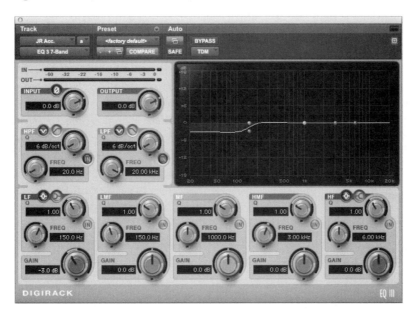

### Harmonic Enhancement

High-end and low-end enhancers, such as the Aphex Aural Exciter and Big Bottom, use a proprietary process that restores or adds to the perception of high- or low-frequency content without increasing level. A number of dance and electronic music artists use these processes on their mixes.

# Dynamic Range Control

## Compression/Limiting

The compressor is perhaps the most misunderstood piece of gear in the studio, largely because it's difficult for the untrained ear to hear exactly what a compressor does. A good compressor well used may not even be discernible in a track. Here's a simple guide to comp/limiters.

A compressor or limiter is used to control the dynamic range of a performance.

What's the difference between a compressor and a limiter? The gain reduction ratio, as in:

< 10:1 = compression
> 10:1 = limiting

What does the ratio relate to? Input to output gain comparison. Look at it this way: assuming your ratio is set at 2:1, if your input signal increases 2 dB above the threshold, your output level will only increase by 1 dB.

At 4:1, for every increase of 4 dB above the input threshold, the output will increase 1 dB.

At 20:1, for every increase of 20 dB on the input, the output will increase 1 dB.

At infinity:1 . . . well, you can do the math.

There are two kinds of compressors, in my opinion: units that are clean, clinical, and fairly transparent sonically; and units that are dirty and distorted and sound amazing if used/abused in the right manner. And of course, there are a few that can do both depending on how you set them up.

While I don't generally believe in "one size fits all" solutions for equipment settings, there is a basic compressor setting that will get you started with just about any recording. This gives you clean dynamic range control without being terribly obvious. It looks like this: 2:1 ratio, 10 ms attack, 150 ms release, set threshold for no more than –6 dB gain reduction. Use it on a vocal track to get it to sit properly in a mix; use it on room mics to get a drum set to sound more aggressive; use it on just about anything to even out dynamics for mixing. Obviously, this won't work in every situation; you wouldn't use this setting on a stereo bus, for example.

Pro Tools comes with an AVIDRack Compressor/Limiter: Dynamics 3.

## Multi-Band Compression

A multi-band compressor is an amalgam of a crossover, an EQ, and a compressor. This handy device allows you to select a frequency band or bands to compress independently of its neighboring frequencies. Used most often in mastering, it can also be used to add final polish to a vocal track, drum track, or anything with complex frequency content that needs to be managed.

One of the great features of multi-band compression is the ability to use different dynamic control settings on each band. You could use a quick attack, quick release setting with GR of –6 dB on the low frequency band; a fast-attack, slow-release setting with GR of –1.5 dB on the mid-range band; and a slow-attack, slow-release setting with –3 dB GR on the high-band. By contrast, a single-band compressor uses one ratio, one attack time, one release time, and one threshold to process all frequencies that pass through the device.

Pro Tools does not include a multi-band compressor in the standard complement of plug-ins. There are a number of great third-party units out there; my personal preference is for the iZotope Ozone 5 (AAX Native) or the WAVES C6 (AAX Native).

## Expanders/Noise Gates

An expander (or downward expansion circuit) is a gentler form of noise gate and is the functional opposite of a compressor. An expander reduces the level of a signal below a threshold, whereas the compressor decreases the level of signal above a threshold.

An expansion ratio of 2:1 will result in a level reduction of 2 dB for every 1 dB below threshold. So a signal drop of 2 dB below threshold would result in a further reduction of 4 dB.

At a 4:1 ratio, the output level would drop –4 dB for every –1 dB below threshold. Hence, a –2 dB drop would result in level reduction of –8 dB on output.

At ratios of 10:1 or higher, the expander becomes a noise gate.

Pro Tools comes with an Expander/Gate that has an optional Look Ahead feature, the purpose of which is not actually to see into the future, but rather to assess the attack time required to preserve transients and to delay the output by that amount.

## De-Essers

Ever notice that your vocal tracksss sseeem ttto have a lot of sssibilance? Use a de-esser plug-in to dynamically control the high frequency saturation on a vocal track when *s*'s and *t*'s are emphatically and vigorously (sp)uttered.

In the absence of a de-esser plug-in, you can construct one using your EQ 3 plug-in and Dynamics 3 plug-in. Place the EQ first in the chain followed by the compressor. Adjust the high-frequency shelf (or notch) to emphasize the problem frequency. (I know, sounds counterintuitive, but hang in there for a minute.) Then use the EQ plug-in to trigger the key input on the compressor. Varying the EQ frequency and amplitude boost, as well as the amount of gain reduction on the compressor, will yield a surprisingly effective method of controlling sibilance in a vocal track. Don't overdo it, or you'll end up with a lisping singer. Great fun at parties, though.

Pro Tools comes with a dedicated De-Esser plug-in as part of the AVIDRack series. Insert this plug-in before you compress or EQ your vocal tracks, or your processing might make the job of de-essing much less effective.

# Pitch Tools

## Pitch Change

A pitch change plug-in is a tool that manipulates samples in time in order to create pitch change, and can be automated to create a dynamic change in a performance. If a sax part has one note that is consistently out of tune, a pitch plug-in can be set to correct the intonation for each occurrence. The AAX AVIDRack plug-in, Pitch II, allows you to raise or lower pitch up to an octave, and works in real-time. This function is automatable.

Note: If you want to make the pitch change more permanent, these effects can also be applied using Audio Suite Pitch Shift processing to create new pitch-altered clips, thereby keeping the real-time host processing demands to a minimum. This can be a great deal of manual work, which brings us to the alternative.

## Pitch Correction

Auto pitch-correction tools have gotten very sophisticated, and can take the automation task out of the hands of the engineer and place it in the realm of the computer and its ability to make lightning-fast calculations to analyze changes in pitch. Using a frequency counter function to determine the half-wave pitch of the note as performed, the plug-in determines the nearest note played, then calculates the pitch change necessary to bring that note into tune. This is a real-time operation and uses a great deal of processing power to accomplish. Examples of auto tuning plug-ins would be:

- **Antares Auto-Tune:** First designed as a stand-alone hardware pitch corrector, this has evolved into a versatile real-time pitch correction tool with numerous editable and automatable parameters. Set it to maximum for the infamous T Pain effect.

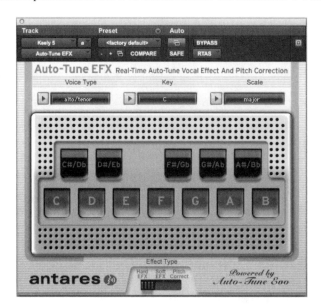

- **Melodyne:** Perfected the art of offline performance editing, now including the ability to edit pitches within a polyphonic performance. This is a virtual laboratory of delights for the serious vocal producer.

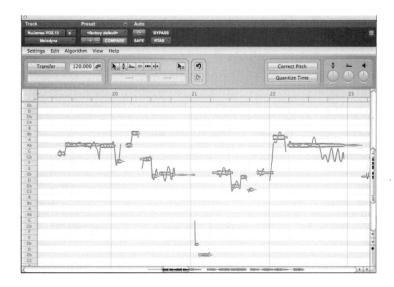

## Creative Use of Pitch Effects

Caution: Use subtly and sparingly. Overuse can cause nausea or motion sickness.

- **Chorus:** To make a chorus effect, take a stereo pitch-change plug-in and set the left-side pitch at +6 cents and the right side at –6 cents. Adjust the mix control to determine the amount of chorus effect. (Reference the Mike Stern school of clean guitar tone.)
- **Harmonies:** Use a mono pitch-change plug-in to add a higher octave to a bass guitar. Set mix control at 50 percent. This is particularly effective when used in a trio setting or sparsely orchestrated song. Try tuning it an octave below when used with a lead guitar part. (Think Prince.) You can set it to other intervals as well for chord or harmony effects.

# Time-Based Effects

## Phase-Reverse

Phase errors can occur when there are minute timing differences between two or more microphones capturing the same sound source. Phase errors are the bane of multitrack recording. A phase reverse plug-in (or activating the phase flip on an EQ or other plug-in) will shift the phase of that signal by 180 degrees, thereby reversing the phase error and eliminating a great deal of unwanted cancellation—or reinforcement—of frequencies when mixing.

To check phase on two tracks, pan them mono and set the track levels the same. Then reverse the phase on one track. You may have a phase problem if:

- The signal drops in level
- The signal increases in level
- A portion of the frequency spectrum gets quieter
- A portion of the frequency spectrum gets louder
- The signal goes away completely

If you encounter any of these problems, you are hearing phase cancellation in the recording. Use the phase reversal function on a short-delay (or other) plug-in to determine the setting that most faithfully represents the sound of the original recorded instrument.

Phase is particularly difficult to control when recording or mixing a drum kit. Good miking practice when recording is just about the only solution to this problem.

Prevention is the best cure, so remember the 3 to 1 rule when recording. (Two microphones must be three times farther from each other than the distance to the sound source when recording.)

Most of the AVIDRack EQ and dynamics plug-ins incorporate a phase reverse button into their designs.

## Reverb

Reverb is the third temporal stage of sound, after direct sound and early reflection. Reverb is a complex series of delays that appear to be indistinct to our ears and give space and depth to sound. Think about the sound you get while bouncing a basketball in a gymnasium. Big halls with long reverb decay times (> 3 seconds) are good for slow songs, vocals, sparse arrangements, or special effects. Rooms with medium decay times (1–3 seconds) are good for general use with all instruments. Plates or small rooms with short decay times (< 1.5 seconds) are good for percussive sounds and up-tempo songs.

Don't forget that bastion of the '80s pop music, the nonlinear reverb, a.k.a. "the Phil Collins drum sound." Phil didn't invent it, but he sure did popularize it. It's still a valid tool, especially when trying to make a snare drum sound bigger in the mix. Just don't overdo it.

Reverbs are usually applied as parallel processing in a send/return configuration using aux tracks. You can use a dedicated reverb plug-in per track, but it will consume lots of CPU cycles by the time you instantiate a reverb plug-in on every track that requires 'verb. It's also easier to change settings on one or two plugs rather than duplicating settings across multiple instances of a reverb plug-in.

Pro Tools ships with a number of reverb plug-ins, including AIR Nonlinear Reverb, AIR Reverb, AIR Spring Reverb, and D-Verb.

## Delay

Delay is a repeated sound, which can be heard as a discrete event occurring a short interval of time after the original event. It can be a single echo or multiple repeats.

- Short delays (< 100 ms) create a doubling effect.
- Medium delays (100–200 ms) are used for slapback delay and tape delay emulation. Think Rockabilly music or some of the classic Sun Records recordings of Elvis, Johnny Cash, Carl Perkins, and so on.
- Long delays (> 200 ms) appear as discrete echoes of the original sound and can be used to lengthen the apparent duration of a sound or performance.
- Pro Tools delay plug-ins give you the option of setting delay times based on tempo and note durations, making it much easier to create musical delay settings without reaching for your calculator.

Pro Tools comes with the following delay plug-ins: AIR Dynamic Delay, AIR Multi Delay, and Mod Delay III.

## Modulation Effects

These are also time-based effects, but the pitch can be dynamically altered by a LFO to produce sweeping effects, such as flanging or chorus.

- Flanging occurs between 2 and 10 ms.
- Chorus effects occur between 10 and 50 ms.

Pro Tools ships with the following modulation effect plug-ins: AIR Chorus, AIR Ensemble, AIR Flanger, AIR Multi Chorus, AIR Phaser, and Sci-Fi.

## Time Compression/Expansion, or TC/E

Used for lengthening or shortening the duration of a file or clip. This can be applied as an Audio Suite process or as an editing function when the Time Compression/Expansion mode is selected for the Trimmer tool.

For obvious reasons, a new file is written when this effect is applied. It gets back to that "no seeing into the future" thing we covered earlier.

# Other Effects

## Distortion

In the world of mixing, distortion occurs when signal processing changes the basic shape of an audio waveform. An example would be the over-modulated clipping of a sine wave resulting in a square wave—a distortion of the original waveform.

Remember when I wrote about learning the rules so you could break them later? Okay, now's your big chance. We usually avoid all types of distortion when recording tracks, but yes, you can use distortion as an intentional effect in the mixing process. It serves multiple duties, because distortion can add harmonic richness, distinctive equalization, and dramatic compression effects, all using one plug-in properly applied. Pro Tools comes with a brilliant guitar amp emulator, called, simply, Eleven. (Google *This Is Spinal Tap*.) It sounds killer on guitar, of course, but it can also lend a dramatic sense of urgency to a variety of other instruments, including vocals.

There are two ways to use distortion effects in your mix:

**Option 1:** Apply the Eleven plug-in as an insert on an aux input, then use aux sends from individual channels to send audio to the plug-in in parallel to the normal output. This allows you to dynamically mix the effect to taste in the context of your mix. The send can also be easily automated.

**Option 2:** Apply the Eleven plug-in directly onto a track insert and tweak until you achieve the perfect amount of distortion for your track. The plug-in parameters can still be automated, but you will not be able to control the balance of un-effected track to effected track quite so easily. This method is good if you want the effect during the entire song and don't need to obsess over the subtleties.

You can try to introduce distortion by overdriving one of your EQ or dynamics plug-ins, but do so cautiously, or it may result in harsh digital clipping. (This is a whole other sonic animal than the pleasing low-order harmonic enhancing effects of a nice tube amp or distortion pedal.) Distortion can be very effective on drum sub-mixes as an enhancement. See *Nine Inch Nails* for reference examples. Trent Reznor is one of a handful of producers who effectively use distortion as a creative tool.

## Other Tools and Plug-ins

### Beat Detective

Beat Detective was originally designed as an automated module to help edit and change the timing of drum parts, primarily. Before Beat Detective, this type of editing was done manually and was a slow and painstaking operation. Now it's easy to fix timing on sections of multiple tracks, change tempos, and change or apply groove characteristics to a live performance using this handy—but fairly complex—module.

The difference between Beat Detective and Elastic Audio is that Elastic Audio uses TC/E to achieve timing and tempo changes, whereas Beat Detective edits a track or tracks into tempo-delineated sub-clips and shifts the timing of those clips according to the current tempo and grid settings.

### Elastic Audio

Okay, AVID has found a way to see into the future. Not enough to get you tomorrow night's lotto numbers, but just enough to change the tempo of a recorded track without altering the pitch. And yes, it happens in real-time.

Elastic Audio changes tempos in real-time by using time compression/expansion (TCE) to achieve dynamic tempo changes.

Pro Tools comes with more than 70 useful and creative plug-ins, which should provide you with hours of entertainment. I have already described a number of the more common plug-ins. The remaining plugs range from metering devices to guitar-amp emulators and virtual instruments. There are also lo-fi plug-ins for sound design applications or creative applications of audio distortion.

### VocALign

This is a third-party software plug-in that compares two similar audio files and adjusts the timing of one audio file to that of another. VocaALign uses TC/E to adjust the destination audio and writes a new file, replacing the destination clip. As this is a third party plug-in, it does *not* come with Pro Tools.

### Panning

*Pan* is the term used to describe the distribution of signal in the panorama between the left and right channels or speakers. In strategizing your mix beforehand, you probably thought about how to present your mix across the pan spectrum. The most common practice in panning is to present the song as it might be heard in a live performance, with instruments panned roughly as they might appear on stage. There are plenty of opportunities to get creative with panning, including automating pan sweeps to tempo or using delays to alternate side to side.

Don't be afraid to use the entire stereo field. You can pan things to the extremes and still be subtle, musical. Season to taste and find the right effect for the song.

# Summary of Key Commands

| Operation | Key Command |
|---|---|
| Keep Plug-in Window Open | Shift + Click – Plug-in Name or Insert Button |
| Copy Plug-in Settings | Shift + Command + C |
| Paste Plug-in Settings | Shift + Command + V |
| Copy Plug-in Assignment | Option + Drag - Plug-in |

# Chapter 4 Review

1.  Audio Suite processing writes a new _____ with the _____ embedded into the clip.
2.  AAX stands for _____ _____ _____ and refers to the proprietary plug-in format for Pro Tools.
3.  You can insert up to ____ plug-ins on each track.
4.  In order to save system resources and free up voices, you may have to make plug-ins inactive by _____ + _____ + _____ on the Insert button associated with the plug-in you wish to deactivate.
5.  The right mouse-click is a timesaver, providing extra menus accessible by clicking around the Edit and Mix windows. How do you access the right-click menu with a one-button mouse? _____.
6.  You can print tracks with effects using two methods. The first is by using _____ plug-ins, and the second is by recording effected clips to another track using an _____ input for routing.
7.  An ____ is a frequency-based tool that allows you to raise or lower the volume of a particular frequency or band of frequencies.
8.  Pro Tools includes a powerful EQ plug-in called EQ 3, which has three different versions available: ___ band, ___ band, and ___ band.
9.  When using EQ on a track, you should try _____ EQ first before using _____ EQ.
10. A well-recorded track should never need EQ. True or False? _____
11. A compression ratio of 8:1 indicates _____, while a ratio of 2:1 indicates _____.
12. A multi-band compressor is a combination of crossover, an EQ, and a compressor, and allows you to selectively compress _____.
13. An expander becomes a noise gate at ratios of _____ or higher.
14. The function of a de-esser is to reduce the _____ in a vocal performance.
15. To correct the pitch, or tuning, of a recorded performance, you can use a manual _____ plug-in for single notes, or an _____ tool such as Antares Auto Tune or Melodyne.
16. _____ is used to correct recorded phase errors between two microphones.
17. Reverb is actually a complex series of _____, which our ears hear as diffuse space.
18. Name the three Pro Tools delay plug-ins:

    _____

    _____

    _____

19. Chorus and flanging are two examples of modulated _____ effects.
20. Adding _____ to a vocal track can be a radical effect, but completely valid in the right context.
21. The Pro Tools module that allows you to quantize recorded performances is known as _____.
22. Panning is an important tool to distribute energy across the _____ field.

# Chapter 5

# UNDERSTANDING AUTOMATION

The automation capability of Pro Tools has always been one of the most convincing reasons to use it as an all-in-one recording and mixing platform. While you can mix from a manual mixing console into your DAW by recording your mix live into an audio track, the *real* power and glory in working with Pro Tools lies in the ability to have the computer memorize and repeat each and every parameter change and nuance of a mix. It is quite simple to edit and refine dynamic automation information in nearly infinite detail. Not to mention the ability to instantly recall the exact same mix—weeks, months, even years later—in order to make revisions.

The scope of this topic is very broad, so I am devoting an entire chapter to automation functions.

Note: Some advanced automation functions are only available in Pro Tools HD. This will be noted in each occurrence.

## Quick-Start Guide to Automation

Getting started with automation is fairly simple; just follow these basic steps:

**Step 1:** Using the Automation window (Window > Automation), enable the types of automation data you plan to record.

**Step 2:** Select the Automation mode on the tracks you plan to automate.

**Step 3:** Hit Play.

**Step 4:** Any changes you make to the enabled controls will be written as automation data, which can be played back, edited, modified, or erased.

Automation data is saved along with your session file.

# Track Parameters That Can Be Automated

## Audio Track Parameters

- Volume
- Volume Trim (Pro Tools HD only)
- Pan
- Mute
- Send Level
- Send Level Trim (Pro Tools HD only)
- Send Pan
- Send Mute
- Plug-in Parameters

## Auxiliary Input Track Parameters

- Volume
- Volume Trim (Pro Tools HD only)
- Pan
- Mute

## Master Fader Parameters

- Volume
- Volume Trim (Pro Tools HD only)

## MIDI Track Parameters

- MIDI Volume
- MIDI Pan
- MIDI Mute
- Continuous Controller Events

## Instrument Track Parameters

- Audio Volume
- Volume Trim (Pro Tools HD only)
- Audio Pan
- Audio Mute

# Recording Real-Time Automation

## Automation Modes

- **Off:** Turns off all automation parameters on the selected track.
- **Read:** Plays automation data written for the track.

- **Write:** Writes new automation data from the point at which playback is started. Overwrites existing automation data.
- **Touch:** Automation data is written only when a fader, switch, or knob is touched, and stops writing when released. Data before and after the touch is unaltered. Overwrites existing data while active.
- **Latch:** Starts writing automation when a fader, switch, or knob is touched, and continues writing until the transport is stopped or the automation mode is changed. Overwrites existing data while active.
- **Trim:** While other automation modes write *absolute* auto data, Trim mode writes *relative* automation data. In other words, when using Trim mode, all of your previously written automation moves remain intact but can be dynamically trimmed louder or softer. This is the perfect solution for raising vocal levels overall by +1 or 2 dB, for example. Note: Trim mode is only available in Pro Tools HD.

## Enabling Automation

Choose the automation control Window > Automation (Command + 4), then click the corresponding buttons to enable the parameters you wish to write to the automation playlists.

From this window, you can also suspend all automation functions and activity, and control Manual Write commands.

For Pro Tools HD users, you also have access to Auto Join and Auto Match controls.

- **Auto Join:** If the transport is stopped in Write mode, Auto Join lets you automatically resume writing in Latch mode.
- **Join:** If the transport is stopped in Write mode, Join lets you manually resume writing in Latch mode. This mode is only available with a supported control surface connected.
- **Auto Match:** When writing automation, use this button to immediately return all automation controls to their previous levels before that pass.
- **Preview Mode:** Allows you to audition changes to an automation pass for all write-enabled controls. The Preview button isolates the control and suspends writing data for that control. If you want to capture the changes, you can punch them in using the down arrow to the right of the Preview button. This gives you the opportunity to rehearse or fine-tune automation moves before committing them to an automation playlist.
- **Capture:** Highlighting a clip or section of a song and then pressing the Capture button copies the current state of all automation parameters, often called an automation *snapshot*. Locating to another part of a song and then clicking the down arrow to the right of the Capture button transfers all of the automation settings in the Capture buffer to the current location. This is a very quick means of copy/pasting automation data within a song.

## Performing an Automation Pass

When you activate the Write-Automation modes, you enable Pro Tools to capture automation data when the state of faders, buttons, or knobs are changed while playing the sequence.

## Plug-in Automation

All plug-ins have automation capability, so you can automate nearly all plug-in parameters.

To enable plug-in controls:

- Open a plug-in window and click the Automation Enable button, or locate the track's Track View selector in the Edit window and Control + Option + Command + Click on it. This will bring up a Plug-in Automation window, which will allow you to enable any or all plug-in parameters to be automated.
- Select the controls you wish to enable, click Add, then click OK to close the window.
- Repeat this step for each plug-in you wish to enable.
- The plug-in window will now show a colored highlight surrounding the parameters you have auto enabled.

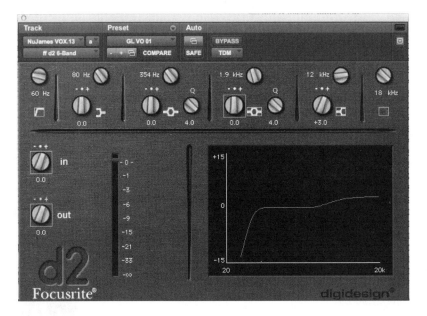

- Whenever you roll the track and adjust one of these parameters, the data will be stored to an automation playlist.

## Auto Safe Mode

Once you're satisfied with the plug-in automation pass you've captured, click the Auto Safe button to keep plug-in automation from being overwritten. Click it again to enable auto writing.

## Viewing and Editing Automation Data

Pro Tools stores automation data in a separate playlist for each track and parameter. This can be viewed and edited as a series of breakpoints, which can be added, deleted, or moved individually or in groups. The information can be viewed as an overlay on the track waveform display, or in a separate lane. The automation lane can be activated by selecting from a drop-down list on the left side of each track.

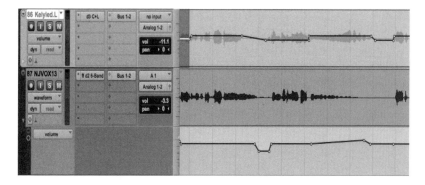

You can view and edit automation data two ways in the Edit window:

1. Choose Track View Select and click on the parameter you wish to view/edit. This displays one parameter at a time.
2. Click on the Lane View Selector in the track you wish to view. This adds a small, scalable lane below the audio track displaying an automation parameter. You can choose which parameter is displayed in the Lane View Selector drop-down menu. You can open as many of these automation lanes as you have parameters to view.

From either of these windows, you can view or edit automation data, which appears as a series of breakpoints connected by a line. Using the cursor and its various Pencil tools, you can edit, add, or delete any automation point you like. The Pencil tool allows you to draw automation data in a variety of shapes, either in free time or locked to the sequence grid settings. Experiment with these Pencil tool settings to create rhythmic panning effects, level effects, mute effects, or just about anything or any parameter you can think of creating.

You can also copy and paste automation data by clip. Automation data can be deleted from these views by simply highlighting the desired clip and hitting the Delete key.

## Thinning Automation

Pro Tools captures the maximum density of automation data available when you write dynamic automation. In a complex mix with many moves, sometimes the amount of data captured can significantly slow system performance on playback. In order to restore system performance while retaining the automation moves, it may be necessary or desirable to thin the automation written. This can be done automatically or manually.

*Smooth and Thin Data After Pass:* This button, located in the Preferences > Mixing pane, gives you the option to automatically thin data after each pass (by selectable degrees) when the button is checked.

*Thin* and *Thin All* Commands: These manual commands allow you to select a track clip and thin the displayed data parameter (Option + Command + T) or thin all automation parameters in the clip (choose Edit > Automation > Thin All).

The *Undo* Command: This command will return automation to its previous unthinned state.

Suggestion: If you apply any of these automation edit commands, A/B the selection to be sure you haven't lost subtle moves vital to your mix.

## Strategies for Automating Your Mix

- Once you have a good rough balance, make a basic pass through the song in Write mode, adjusting the general shape of the mix levels.

- Continue to refine your mix a section at a time, or a track (or group of tracks) at a time, using Touch mode.
- With plug-ins in place and adjusted, make dynamic changes as necessary or desired by enabling automation parameters on the plug-in page.
- If your computer gets sluggish or won't play back your automation, it's possible that you have generated a large amount of automation data by capturing dynamic changes. In which case, you should review and thin the data to make sure your computer can process the data effectively.

### Trim Mode

When you have arrived at a satisfactory mix, fine adjustments can be made using Trim mode. This data can be easily modified or deleted to reveal your original mix data. Use Trim mode for the last 1 percent of changes to your mix to create the perfect balance.

## Working with Control Surfaces

While each control surface is worthy of its own book, I will briefly discuss the merits of using these devices to extend the capabilities of Pro Tools by giving you immediate and simultaneous availability of many more parameters than you could possibly access using your mouse and keyboard alone.

Note: Control Surfaces do not usually include I/O devices, so you will need to connect sufficient I/O for your session needs.

There are a good number of compatible control surfaces available for use with Pro Tools. For the purpose of this book, we will take a general look at two popular systems, the AVID C|24 and the Euphonics EuCon Artist Series.

## AVID C|24

The C|24 is a fixed-form (not expandable) control surface using 24 moving faders and a dedicated analog monitor section. This is a mid-level, self-contained console solution for engineers requiring many of the features of a traditional analog console, including multiple speaker selections, headphone outputs, talkback functions, multiple input monitoring, plus 16 built-in mic preamps/line/DI inputs.

Each of the 24 virtual channels has dedicated buttons to control Mute, Solo, Record, Select, EQ, Dynamics, Insert, Send, and Automation functions.

- The touch-sensitive fader encoders make it easy to write or update automation passes by simply grabbing the motorized fader and making dynamic level changes in real-time.
- Even though there are 24 physical faders, the C|24 is capable of accessing any number of Pro Tools tracks by changing banks up or down. An LED scribble strip lets you know what's on each fader in that bank.
- The C|24 encoders are 10-bit resolution for accurate data capture, which is interpolated to 24-bits on playback.

## EuCon

When AVID purchased console manufacturer Euphonics in 2010, they brought a wide range of consoles and control surface options to the massive Pro Tools install base. Almost immediately, AVID announced the Artist Series control surfaces, including the Artist Control and Artist Mix modular mixer components.

I installed both the Artist Control and an Artist Mix module for the purpose of illustrating the benefits of mixing with a control surface.

Setup of the modules requires the installation of EuControl software, which senses the availability and identity of EuCon modules when the system is booted. Once the system recognizes that the modules are powered up and connected (via Ethernet cables), you must set up Pro Tools to recognize the modules. In the Preferences pane, you will be able to access the Ethernet Controller page and activate the EuCon functionality with a single mouse-click.

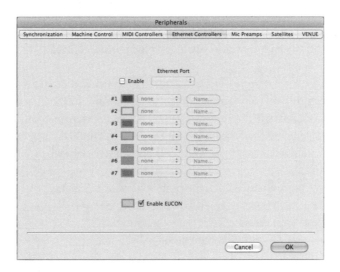

- The Artist Control has four motorized faders with Function buttons and a dedicated transport control, as well as a plethora of soft button controls on a user-definable touch screen.
- The Artist Mix offers a bank of eight motorized faders with Function buttons and an LED scribble strip for track identification.
- A great thing about working with the Artist Series is the amount of parameter control you get in a relatively small footprint. In a space roughly 10" x 20" x 1.5", you can control an infinite number of Pro Tools tracks (or other DAW software, video editing software, and so forth). By using bank commands from the control surface, you are able to control groups, VCA faders, or individual tracks at your fingertips—plus edit commands, disk commands, and more. And of course, it's expandable up to 36 faders.
- The dedicated parameter encoders give you instant access to plug-in parameter control and are fully automatable.
- One of the most convenient aspects of using a control surface relates to writing automation. Growing up on an analog console gives me an appreciation for grabbing a handful of faders and feeling my way through a mix. With a control surface, you can perform a preliminary automation pass by feel, then go back and fine-tune your moves with unprecedented levels of precision.
- EuCon encoders use 12-bit resolution for a high degree of parameter capture/playback accuracy.

# Summary of Key Commands

| Operation | Key Command |
|---|---|
| Automation Control Window | Command + 4 |
| Plug-in Automation Window | Control + Option + Command + Click – Insert Button |
| Thin Automation Data | Option + Command + T |

# Chapter 5 Review

1. The main automatable audio track parameters include:
   _____, _____, _____, _____.
2. The Automation modes are various ways to handle automation data. Four of the modes are: _____, _____, _____, _____.
3. The Automation window allows you to enable multiple controls. This window can be accessed by using _____ + ___.
4. Nearly every plug-in parameter can be automated using the plug-ins _____ _____ menu. This menu can accessed by selecting it in the Plug-in window.
5. Auto Safe mode refers to the state of a plug-in protected from automation _____. This is enabled using the Safe button on the Plug-in window.
6. It can be advantageous to _____ Pro Tools automation data when automating a large or complex mix.
7. The two ways to view auto data in the Edit window are by using Track View Select and choosing the _____ parameter, and by activating one of the _____ _____ using the Lane View Selector below the audio track.
8. A good way to refine your mix automation is by using _____ mode to fine-tune your automation moves.

# Chapter 6

# THE ART AND SCIENCE OF THE MIX

Let's take a look at some of the creative and technical decisions you'll be facing in the mixing process.

## The Weakest Link—Recording Quality vs. Final Results

Here's an axiom to consider carefully: Your mix will only sound as good as the original recording. If your original recording/performance quality is poor, chances are you won't get the greatest results in your mix. A common misconception is that you can "fix it in the mix." While a nifty rhyme, it's not a good philosophy for making great music. (Frank Zappa famously said, "We'll fix it in the shrinkwrap.") Taking a few extra minutes and a little more care in the recording process can literally save you hours in the mix. In other words: garbage in, garbage out. You can't polish a turd, etc.

## Musical Styles/Genres

Mixing a classical recording requires different tools and a different approach than does mixing hip-hop, so you should prepare for your session accordingly. Listen to well-known projects to familiarize yourself with the common palette of techniques used in mixing for that genre. Think about how hip-hop mixers approach compression and EQ differently than rock or pop mixers. There are many engineer interviews available online via MixOnline.com and TapeOp.com. Study up on processing techniques, and then try new ideas in your own mixes. This is how you build your toolkit.

Note: Mixing a live recording usually requires a fair amount of setup and processing in order to get the best results.

# Editing for Content

Editing for content falls more into the realm of producing or arranging, but there may be times when a song needs a little help with arranging or form or groove. Mixing your own material gives you one last opportunity to examine the form of the song—Is it too long? Can the intro or solo be edited out? Does the second verse actually work better as a first verse? What about a breakdown to bass and vocal in the third chorus? This is a great time to get experimental to find out what a new perspective on the arrangement might bring to the music.

Note: As a mixer working on someone else's recording, you need to exercise some restraint before you chop the song into little pieces and reassemble it and add loops and a rap section. Develop a rapport with your client so you understand one another's needs and goals. Who knows, if you're good at it you could make a name for yourself as a re-mixer.

# Mixing "In the Box" vs. Mixing on a Console

There are advantages to each method as well as disadvantages, but let's be sure we're considering the *real* pluses and minuses before declaring one method good and the other . . . not so much. Mixing "in the box" means handling all of your level changes, panning, and signal processing within the host application, using no external audio mixing console or processing gear.

The other option is mixing on a console, using Pro Tools as a playback device only. All leveling, panning, EQ, dynamics, and other processing would be done using the console and/or outboard gear.

You can employ a hybrid version of these methods by sub-mixing Pro Tools tracks to sub-masters, then mixing those sub-masters on a console. You can also use external compression, EQ, or other processing in a send/return configuration. This gives you the power of combining Pro Tools automation with the sonic integrity of your vintage outboard kit. You may find that different songs each require a different approach in order to achieve the desired results. Experiment; figure out which method works best for you.

# Tracksheets/Documentation

If you've followed good mental hygiene and named all of your tracks during the session, then your job will be much easier at the mixing stage. There's nothing more frustrating than weeding through 72 tracks named "Audio 1," "Audio 96," etc. If a session comes to you for mixing that looks like this, take the time to decipher which track is which and name it accordingly. It'll make your life so much easier when you're looking for the right background vocal part among 50-plus takes across two dozen tracks.

Keep notes on important aspects of a recording, either in the Comments field in a Pro Tools track or in a separate text document, so you can identify cool things (or problems that may need attention) when it comes time to mix.

# Keeping Track of Mix Sessions and Mix Files

Pro Tools allows you to keep many sequences within the session folder that also contains your audio files, fade files, video files, and sequence backups. It's important to keep all materials related to your session together in one place so you can re-create the session at a later date.

Keep track of your hard disk usage; if the disk becomes too full, you may not be able to write fade files or save sequences to the original session folder. In this case, you should consider copying the entire session folder to a new hard drive or partition with sufficient capacity to finish your work. This is accomplished by using the "Save copy in . . . " command in the File menu at the top of your screen.

# Naming Conventions

When recording, name tracks using the instrument or part first, then include other identifying info—e.g., Vocal Lead, Vocal Verse, Vocal Chorus, etc. Or, Guitar Solo, Guitar Acoustic Rhythm, Guitar Squawking Noises, and so on. If you follow this method, all of your recorded clips will show up in the Clips list in alphabetical order, making it much easier to locate all of the guitar parts, then find the subset of takes you're searching for.

If you are given a session to mix that uses the default "Audio 1" naming scheme, you must decide whether or not to take the time to rename all clips (i.e., *forever*), consolidate all clips on a track into one file with an appropriate name (time consuming but worth it), or leave the clips alone and identify them by color and memory.

If tracks are clearly named, that may be sufficient for you to work with; however, locating an alternate background vocal or guitar take can be a challenge if the original engineer has spread takes across multiple shared tracks.

# Data Management

Save session versions that correspond with their mixed files. Since you can (and should) keep all of your sequence files in your session folder, it's important to be able to identify your session files as they relate to your mixes. I save a new version of a sequence every time I make a major change to the song or mix. There may be five or six versions of an edit before I even get to the first mix, but the name of the first mix file *always* corresponds to the name of the sequence. For example, if I've edited five versions of Song A and saved that version of the sequence as "Song A Edit 05," the mix resulting from that sequence will be titled "Song A Mix 05."

Why? Two reasons:

1) If my clients love the vocal mix on Version 05 but really want the edited guitar solo from Version 03, I need to be able to quickly locate and identify the sequence elements in order to give them the mix they want.

2) Text characters don't cost anything but the time it takes to type them. If you name your files sequentially, it will be way easier to keep track of everything and not have to rely on your memory when looking through files named "Good Mix" and "OK PNO" and "Sequence 13."

If you view your files alphabetically and use the binary numbering system (01, 02, . . 27, . . . 99, and so forth), then your first version will always be at the top of the file stack, above Version 27 and Version 99.

Find a naming system that works for you and stick to it.

# Keep an Eye on the Final Delivery Medium

Always consult with your mastering engineer to see which file types and formats he or she prefers to work with. Most engineers can accept any format in any configuration, but many have preferences that will make the process faster and simpler. Usually they will ask for the highest possible sample and bit rate, depending on your original session settings.

If you are delivering files for inclusion on a CD, your mix file format should be dithered 16-bit 44.1 kHz Stereo Interleaved AIFF.

Online distribution services have various delivery specifications; these change from time to time, so check with each outlet to determine current delivery specs. The iTunes standard file format is a 256 kbps AAC file, which is a fairly compressed format. This file, like MP3 files, uses data compression to make files smaller. While you have the option to make files that have a higher bit rate (and result in higher fidelity), it should be noted that all AAC, MP3, WMV, and AC3 files use data compression, thereby changing the sound of the original uncompressed, full bandwidth, linear PCM files that you created for your high-quality mix.

# P&E DAW Session Guidelines Document

The Recording Academy (aka the Grammy® people) has a special organization of members dedicated to the technical trade. This group is the Producers and Engineers Wing. Besides providing ongoing professional education and advocacy on behalf of all music makers, the P&E Wing has developed a series of guidelines and recommendations documents designed to help standardize workflow for professional engineers and enthusiasts alike. Of particular interest to Pro Tools users is the *DAW Session Guidelines* document, which discusses standard ways to name tracks, files, and sessions, and includes many helpful tips for keeping your work organized.

Check it out at www.ProducersAndEngineers.com. Look for the link on the right labeled *Guidelines and Recommendations*.

# P&E Master Delivery Document

While you're on the P&E website, download and read the *Master Delivery Recommendations* document as well. This will explain the official specs for delivering your final project to a record label or other Intellectual Property (IP) owner.

## P&E Wing

And since you're already there, you should consider joining the Recording Academy! It's a great way to meet music makers, expand your professional network, and (if you qualify) vote on the Grammy Awards.

# Basic Approaches to Mixing

It's good to have a strategy for mixing: an overarching view of what you plan to do and what your desired outcome will be. There are two basic ways to approach working on a mix: building a house and sculpting.

# Building a House (of *Rock*)

Start with the foundation. This method uses a layered approach to building a mix. Usually I start with the rhythmic instruments and other instruments that occupy the low frequency register, and work my way up through the arrangement, finally adding the vocals at the end to complete the picture. Let's take a look at this method for mixing rock/pop/jazz/country music one instrument at a time.

## Drums

It's not always about the drums. Except in popular music. Pat Metheny once expressed that if the drummer is having a good day, the whole band sounds better. I would paraphrase that to say: If the drums sound good the whole mix sounds better. If you're mixing rock or pop, country or hip-hop, the drums (or beats) are the foundation on which the rest of the mix is built. Paying special attention to the drum sounds will improve the overall sound and feel of your mix.

Depending on the song, getting good drum sounds can be one of the bigger challenges to the quality of your mix. If you get the drums right, the rest of the musical puzzle pieces will fall into place much more easily.

Here is a detailed method for handling drum tracks in your mix.

Line up your tracks in the Edit window like so:

**Track 1:** Kick

**Track 2:** Snare

**Track 3:** High Hat

**Tracks 4–6:** Tom Toms

**Tracks 7–8:** Overhead Mics

**Tracks 9–10:** Room Mics

If you have additional kick, snare, or tom tracks, just put them in order and label them descriptively. (Kick Inside, Kick Outside, Snare Top, Snare Bottom, Tom 1, Tom 2, or Rack Tom, Floor Tom, and so forth.)

This track order lets you work on components of a drum kit in order of *groove priority* (my term). The drum tracks should appear at the top the vertical stack in the Edit window, and at the left-most side of the mixer in the Mix window. This becomes your foundation, and is easy to locate as you work progressively through the mix.

This would be a good time to start thinking about using color coding for your instruments and groups to make them easier to locate. By double-clicking in the color bar area next to the highlighted track name(s), a color-option pop-up window will give you access to a series of color controls. You can set the color of one or more tracks, a track group, or clips in a track along with other options to modify the look of your Edit and Mix windows.

See the Color Palette section for more details.

**Step 1:** Get a general balance of the drum tracks so that you can hear all the tracks equally well.

**Step 2:** Edit the individual tracks so that there is no additional noise at the beginning or end of the track. Take a few moments to edit out the count-off at the beginning and any other chat that happens at the end of the take.

**Step 3:** Apply any EQ or compression as necessary to get the individual tracks to sound their best. Use other musical references to be sure you know what your goal is. Keep some reference tracks available for listening; you may even want to import tracks into your session to make direct comparisons to your mix.

**Step 4:** Create a track group consisting of all the drum tracks. Highlight the track names, then type Command + G, then type the name "Drums." Exclude the room mics (if you have them) from this group since they will likely be treated with different effects than the rest of the kit. This will make it easier to edit the tracks, adjust and automate levels, solo/mute the kit, and generally treat the entire drum kit as a single instrument. If you want to be color coordinated, double-click in the color field to the left of the track name and choose a single color for this group of tracks. It will be easier to identify the drum tracks at a glance if you do. Plus it'll look hipper.

**Step 5a:** Create a new stereo auxiliary track; this will become the destination for your DRUM SUBMIX bus. Here's how you do it: Click on the Output button on the last drum track in the group, mouse down to the "new track . . ." menu. From the Width drop-down menu, select Stereo; in the Type menu, select Aux Input; in the Time Base menu, select either Samples or Ticks, whichever is applicable to your session; and name the track DRUM SUBMIX. (Why all caps? It'll be easier to find as you scroll through dozens of tracks titled in lowercase.) Tick the button labeled "Create next to current track," then click the Create button.

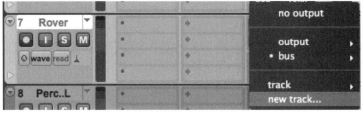

Note: In Pro Tools the input DRUM SUBMIX will already be selected when the new aux track is created. Champion!

**Step 5b:** Select all the drum tracks by name, then press Shift + Option + Click on the Output pane of one of the tracks. Select the DRUM SUBMIX bus.

**Step 6:** Select a compressor plug-in for the first insert slot on the DRUM SUBMIX track. For this exercise, let's use the BF76 Compressor plug-in. Adjust the controls to match those in the figure.

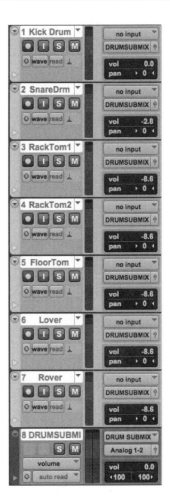

## Editing Drum Tracks

You may find it necessary at some point to edit some of the drum tracks in order to fix timing issues or remove noises. Just be careful not to change the timing of one of the drum tracks without changing the others. See the example under the "Manual Editing" section for two different methods to clean up tom tom tracks.

## Time Aligning Room Tracks

Since you have already located the Room Mic tracks just below the overhead tracks in the Edit window, it should be easy to zoom in and see if the waveforms are aligned. Chances are, the room mics were placed 10 or more feet from the drum kit and will result in the "flamming" of every hit when played back with the rest of the kit. This is because you hear every hit 10 to 30 ms later on the room tracks.

Here's a Pro Tools editing technique you can use to rectify the time alignment issues and add extra power and depth to your drum sounds.

**Step 1:** Create a new Stereo Audio track (Shift + Command + N) and drag the two room mic clips into the new track, which you will then name "Room Mics Stereo." This allows you to access and edit both tracks as one, saving time and CPU cycles. (Note: This can also be helpful when working with other tracks that were recorded as mono tracks but need to be edited or processed as a single stereo track.)

**Step 2:** Zoom in to see how far apart the waveform transients appear on the room tracks as compared to the overheads.

Grab the room mic clip and slide it so that the transient edges match up with the overheads. You can also nudge the tracks into place by setting your nudge factor to 10 ms and using the comma (,) or period (.) keys to nudge left or right in 10 ms increments. Use a finer setting, such as 1 ms, to nudge clips more precisely. Remember, the "M" and "/" keys move clips 10 times the Nudge setting.

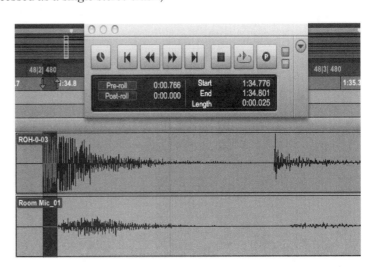

**Step 3:** Mix to taste. You will get all of the live sound goodness of the room mics, but now all the attacks will occur in the right places.

**Step 4:** Optional—Insert an EQ on the Stereo Room Mics track to tailor the frequency response of those tracks. You might find it handy to diminish some of the mid-range frequency content around 400 Hz.

**Step 5:** Optional—Insert a compressor on the track to increase the intensity of the room effect. This is where you can get that trashy "garage" sound that really gives the drum track some energy. Not so much if it's a gentle ballad.

Adding a distortion plug-in or a guitar amplifier emulator such as Eleven or SansAmp could lead to interesting results. Experiment with different settings and plug-ins to get unique effects.

### EQ on Drum Tracks

This is a pretty subjective area and really depends on how well the drums were recorded. Or not. The descriptions below assume that the drum tracks were well recorded to begin with. Always use your ears and your own sensibilities to determine if you need EQ and, if so, to what degree.

### Kick Drum EQ

It's important to reserve a portion of the low end of the frequency spectrum for the kick—separate from the bass track. Allowing those frequencies to overlap will make the low end sound muddy and indistinct.

Using the 5-band EQ 3, set up the low band for a narrow peak curve, set the amplitude for +3 dB, then sweep the low frequencies between 20 Hz and 100 Hz to find the spot that most emphasizes the extreme low end of the kick drum sound. If you have mid-field speakers, you should hear the result clearly.

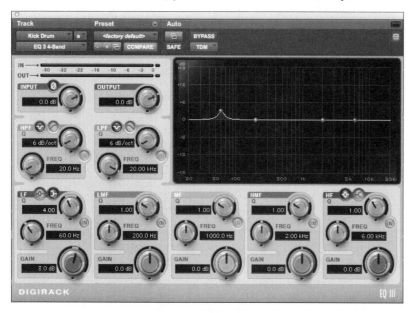

Note: The smaller the kick drum, the higher the frequency center, thereby pushing it up into the bass range. Be careful not to emphasize the same frequencies that make up the fundamental pitches of the bass track. This results in too much low-end energy and will force you to reduce the level of the EQ in that band later in the process.

Using the lower mid-band of the EQ 3 in wide peak mode, set the amplitude for +6 dB and sweep the mids between 250 Hz and 1 kHz to find the hot spot. This frequency will sound remarkably louder than others when you reach it. (It sounds icky, like the box the drum came in.) When you locate that frequency, use that as your target, then adjust the amplitude setting to –6 dB. You will notice a major change in the kick drum sound, and you will hear much more clarity in the instruments occupying the neighboring frequencies.

If you need more of the attack or beater sound from the kick, you can sweep the upper mid-band of the EQ 3 as above to find the frequency that gives you more of that attack. It will typically be somewhere between 1 kHz and 10 kHz.

I know that's a broad range, but no two kicks are alike, and I wasn't there when you recorded yours. I was there when the kick drum in this exercise was recorded, and I can tell you that it also depends on the mic used to capture the sound. This recording was made using an AKG D112, which has a bit of presence rise around 3 kHz and increased sensitivity below 100 Hz. You may find it unnecessary to increase the extreme low end very much, if at all. There is plenty there in the recording.

## Snare EQ

Snare drums have energy all across the frequency spectrum, depending on the drum and the drummer. The key here is to get the snare to occupy a space in the mix that is well defined, yet stays out of the way of other instruments.

A good place to start is to insert a 5-band EQ 3 plug-in on the snare track, then ascertain the one or two frequencies at which a snare drum has the most impact without obscuring other tracks. Since snare drums are all about the initial attack, try to isolate and enhance the sound of the snare strainer wires. This is a high-frequency sound, probably in the vicinity of 4 kHz or above. Sometimes +6 dB of 10 kHz shelf EQ is just right. Listen in context with the other drums. Season to taste.

Some drums, such as piccolo snares, have a sound that makes them easy to feature in a mix because they are so identifiable. Occasionally, this can work against you. For example, a five-inch-deep snare drum with a tightly tuned head can sometimes generate a loud "honk" overtone at around 1 kHz. This might be cool for a grunge tune, but if it sticks out in a mix or if the pitch is too distinct, you may need to do some EQ surgery to get it to behave.

Try sweeping a notch filter across the spectrum until you find the frequency where the honk is diminished or goes away. Make sure the notch doesn't carve too much out of neighboring frequencies, or it may become hard to hear the snare in the mix when the other instruments are added.

Sometimes a snare will need some bottom end added in order to fill out the sound. Try using a peak EQ band on the EQ 3 to add +3 dB at 150 Hz. That should give more body to the snare sound without interfering with the kick drum.

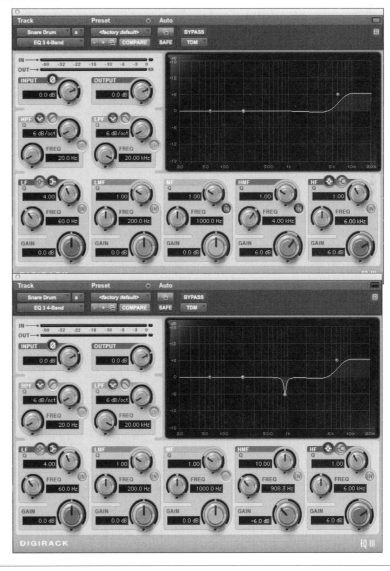

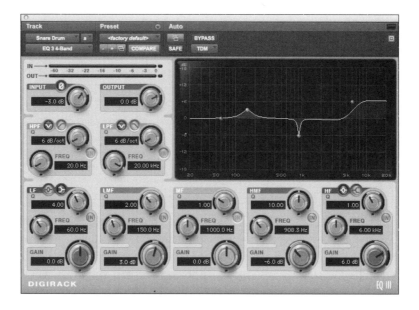

## Dynamics Processing on Drum Tracks

There are two main reasons to use dynamics processors on individual drum tracks: 1) to smooth out the dynamics of an uneven performance, and 2) to tighten up the sound of a kick or snare drum and make for a more energetic kick/snare relationship within the mix. The first example is easy to comprehend; the second scenario needs a bit of explanation.

How can controlling dynamics lead to a more energetic-sounding record? Seems counterintuitive at first. If you remember the exercise where we used a compressor on the room mic tracks, you will recall that the net result of compressing a recorded track is to limit the amplitude of the peak transients while increasing the amplitude of the quieter material in between hits. Compressing the kick makes each hit roughly equal in volume, and compressing the snare brings up all of the quieter detail in the performance (all the stuff in between the big backbeat hits). In addition, by compressing the initial transient, you get a drum sound that sustains longer than the hundred or so milliseconds of natural decay. Hence, you get bigger, badder sounding drums.

Using the Dynamics 3 plug-in will give you very clean dynamic range control without a lot of tonal coloration. If you want to hear tonal coloration, try the BF76 plug-in using the setting titled "All buttons in." Control the amount of limiting by increasing or decreasing the input volume, then compensate by adjusting the output control to get back to nominal output volume. You will hear the difference almost immediately.

# Bass

## Editing Bass Parts

Depending on the accuracy of the original performance, you may wish to adjust the timing of certain bass notes to line up with the kick drum hits. This is entirely dependent on the type of music and the artistic goals of the artist and producer.

Timing can be adjusted using the same waveform comparison technique we used in adjusting the timing of the room mics in the previous exercise. In this instance, we will only be moving certain notes, most likely.

Drag the recorded bass track (or tracks) up underneath the kick drum tracks and play through the song, listening for errors or timing issues. When you find something that sounds out of sync, zoom in (using the T key command) so that the bass note in question can be compared visually with the kick drum track. If you can hear an error, I guarantee you will see a difference.

Once located, you need to decide who's out. If it's the bass, no problem—just isolate the note by selecting a clip consisting of just that note (if possible), and using the Separate Clip command (Command + E), then nudge or move the clip until it appears to be in time with the kick drum. Audition the edit by backing up a few seconds and playing across your edit. If the bass and kick sound better, then it worked. If not, move it back where it was (Undo) or use the Heal command (Command + H) to restore the clip to its original state.

If the problem lies with the drum performance, the process for fixing the timing is the same, but the operation is more complex because you must select *all* of the drum tracks, including the room mics, before you perform the separate/move operation. One drum track out of sync with the rest of the kit makes for a terrible-sounding performance, and potentially a lot of work to fix. Remember—Undo and Save are our friends.

Pro Tools has a Revert to Saved Session option in the event you can't *undo* your way back to a better sync state.

## Bass EQ

This is dependent on the sound of the instrument and the player. Be cognizant of the similarity in fundamental frequency response between the bass and the kick drum; try to shift the emphasis on the bass EQ a little higher than the kick. For example, if you tweak the kick drum +3 dB @ 40 Hz using a peak EQ, you may want to focus on bass frequencies above 100 Hz and roll off information below 50 Hz. There is also a tendency for basses to record with a shortage of information between 1 kHz and 3 kHz. You won't find fundamental frequencies that high, but a lot of the initial attack and clarity comes from that range in the bass. Try adding +3 dB @ 1 kHz next time you find that the bass part is not cutting through the mix.

If there are more than two electric guitar parts in your mix, you may want to consider ducking some of the bass by –3 dB @ 250 Hz just to clear out that portion of the frequency spectrum a bit. This will give the guitars a little space when their parts are played on the lower strings. It's all about separation—whether it's panning or EQ, every instrument needs some space.

## Bass Dynamics Processing

Some basses just sound better in the mix with a little compression. Particularly if you're going for that '60s–'70s era Carol Kaye "Wrecking Crew" sound or the McCartney Beatle-Bass vibe. Try using the BF76 compressor set on 4:1 ratio, fast attack, medium release, and adjust the input gain so that the gain reduction meter is riding at a pretty consistent –3 dB. The tonal coloration introduced by the compressor will even change the relationship of the bass to the other instruments from an EQ perspective, tending to emphasize the low to mid frequencies.

A totally different approach is called for when working with jazz or R&B bass parts. Most R&B bass players I encounter would prefer to use *no* compression whatsoever on their parts. Since I usually record without compression, that's not a problem. When it

comes time to mix a song with a slappin', thumbin', poppin' bass part, you will likely need to tame some of those powerful attack transients. Not like the '60s version above but rather a more surgical approach to dynamic range control that is sonically transparent. In this case, use the Dynamics 3 set on 2:1 ratio, 20 ms attack, 250 ms release, soft-knee curve, with threshold set for no more than –3 dB gain reduction. You will still have all the life and energy of the part as originally played, but now your outputs won't clip when things really get cooking.

Here's another method of locking the bass to the kick track using dynamics: Insert a noise gate plug-in on the bass track and use the Side Chain/Key function to trigger it from the kick drum.

Obviously, if the bass part is busier than the kick drum, you will be gating a lot of bass notes unnecessarily. In which case, you may find it useful to automate the noise gate bypass to turn off the effect when the bass part is more active or there are no timing issues. Next, automate the noise gate to turn on whenever there is a timing issue.

You can use this side chain/key technique with a compressor instead of a noise gate in order to duck the bass level momentarily during each kick hit. This makes the kick drum part stand out more and may appear to clean up the low end of the frequency spectrum by removing the bass track from competition in that register.

## Guitar (GTR)

Ah, guitars. My personal delight. Let's look at how to handle acoustic and electric guitars.

Acoustic guitars can perform a couple of different functions in a band performance, either as a melodic or a rhythmic element (or what I like to call tunable percussion).

## Acoustic Guitar Dynamics Processing

Acoustics love to be compressed—not too much, but just enough. Try using the Dynamics 3 compressor set on 4:1 ratio, 50 ms attack, 250 ms decay, Gain Reduction (GR) of no more than –3 dB. The slightly delayed attack time allows the picking transients to come through unaffected, while the compression tends to make single notes sustain just a bit longer at full volume. This setting should help the guitar sit well in the mix.

## Acoustic GTR EQ

Acoustic guitars have a tendency to produce more low-end information than you need in a mix, so be prepared to insert an EQ 3 7-band plug-in on the acoustic track and reduce the amplitude of the low-shelf EQ –3 dB at around 150 Hz. This will reduce the muddiness of a dreadnaught-style guitar and help keep it out of the bass frequency range. You may find it necessary to use the High-Pass Filter (HPF) to roll off more of the low end: start at 60 Hz and sweep upward to about 100 Hz and stop where the low end cleans up and all the other instruments are audible.

If your acoustic has old strings on it, you can make them sound a bit newer by adding +3 dB with a 10 kHz shelf EQ.

In a complex mix, it's helpful to pan an acoustic guitar track hard left or right to achieve more separation without having to make the track louder. Pan the track opposite of the high hat or shaker to maintain separation.

Electric guitars can be rhythmic, melodic, low end, high end, clean, or distorted, sometimes changing every bar of a performance.

There is no standard formula for effects on electric guitar tracks, and many guitarists hit the studio with their signature sound dialed in and ready to roll using their own rack gear or stomp box pedals.

## Electric GTR Dynamics Processing

If you are mixing a guitar recorded without effects, or maybe just through an amp without processing, you might want to consider compressing that track in the mix. Using the Dynamics 3 plug-in, set the ratio at 3:1, the attack at 20 ms, the release at 150 ms, and adjust the threshold for about –6 dB gain reduction. This will make the clean guitar track loud enough to be heard but not overpower other instruments or vocals. This will help you balance and will save you a lot of automation moves.

Heavily distorted electric guitars are already very compressed, so you shouldn't need to add more. If there is a lot of gain, there will likely be a lot of noise amplified along with it. A properly adjusted noise gate will eliminate the noise in between notes or phrases and allow all of the fuzzy goodness to come through in the right places. Use the Dynamics 3 plug-in set for noise gate only.

### Electric GTR EQ

If you succumb to the temptation to double or triple track all of your electric guitars, you will eventually get to the point where the layers all blend together and become a homogenous mass of guitar goo. In order to hear all the great parts on your arrangement, you may need to use an EQ to reduce some of the low- to mid-band frequencies just to make room for all of those parts. You will probably find a buildup of information around 250–400 Hz. Insert an EQ 3 and cut that frequency with a peak EQ set to a one-octave bandwidth. Start out by cutting –3 dB and sweep the spectrum to find the frequency band that cleans up the guitar sound.

Consider panning doubled tracks symmetrically in your mix (like –50/+50, or –20/+20). This will separate the tracks sonically and give the impression of greater breadth across the pan spectrum.

## Keyboard Tracks

### Synths

Modern keyboard patches come out compressed, EQ'd, and already hyped to the max. You may find it necessary to confine some sounds to specific frequency ranges in order to make them fit into the big picture. Compare the sound of the keys to the other chord instruments to see where some EQ cuts might help the keys fit in.

### Acoustic Piano

Acoustic piano parts are a different story. While some sampled pianos are pre-processed in the box, real pianos are most definitely not. They have a broad range of frequencies and a broader range of dynamics. Each piano has its own personality as well, and a console piano records very differently than a nine-foot Steinway. A nine-foot Steinway sounds very different than a nine-foot Yamaha, and so on.

Once you decide the role of the piano in your mix, you may have to emphasize some high frequencies or add compression in order to achieve your goal. Start out conservative with your effects and work your way up to radical. Always listen to the track with the other chord instruments and the bass to be sure all parts are easily heard.

Many of the classic Motown records were recorded using an upright piano doubled or tripled. Often, these are compressed to reduce the initial attack and increase the apparent sustain. For an old-school sound, try using a BF76 compressor set on 8:1 ratio, medium attack time, medium release time, GR of no more than –6 dB.

## Organs

It's easy to fit a Farfisa or Vox Jaguar into your mix; they have unique sonic signatures that have a pretty narrow bandwidth. A B-3 or other Hammond-type organ with a Leslie rotating speaker is another animal entirely, particularly if the organist is kicking bass pedals. This instrument—like piano—can occupy almost the entire frequency spectrum, so you will need to balance it in the mix primarily using level control.

You might find it interesting to use a distortion effect or guitar amp emulator plug-in on the organ. Listen to Keith Emerson of ELP, or John Lord of Deep Purple—they created classic rock organ sounds that you can use as inspiration for creating your own new sounds.

# Other Instruments

## Percussion

Tambourine: Plenty of high end on these instruments, and huge attack transients as well. If you're looking for a tambo to augment a snare part, don't do too much to the track. If it's a stand-alone eighth- or sixteenth-note part, you may want to compress the part to even out the volume levels.

Shakers provide lots of high end too. Shakers are a good complement to a high hat part, sound great without compression, and fit well into a mix when panned opposite the high hat.

Conga/bongos/djembe/other hand drums: Conga and djembe occupy low–mid frequencies, while bongos tend to fill mid- and upper-midrange frequencies. Huge dynamic swings can benefit from parallel compression. Try using a Maxim plug-in to even out the average performance level and bring up the quiet parts, then use the balance fader to let some of the transient attacks back into the performance. This will keep the part audible and natural sounding without killing your peak meters and clipping the output.

## Mandolin/Banjo/Ukulele

These stringed instruments are similar in that they are tuned higher than acoustic guitars but tend to have less sustain when picked, strummed, or fingered. Sonically, they each have a different range of harmonics, so you will treat each one independently—particularly if they appear together in the same song.

Be cognizant of the tendency of the peak transients to really pop out of a mix. If it serves the rhythm of the song (and if the parts are played in time), this should be a great complement to the other rhythm parts. If the parts stick out too much, you can compress them lightly in order to tame the transients. We're talking maybe –3 dB of gain reduction.

Try panning these opposite an acoustic guitar part for more separation.

## Vocals

Well-recorded vocals usually require little in the way of processing during a mix; 60 Hz high-pass filter (HPF), light compression (no more than –3 dB GR), and a tiny dusting of high-end EQ, administered in the form of +3 dB @16 kHz using the high shelf on an EQ 3.

Then again, if this is aggressive rock/punk/rap, don't be afraid to smack the compressor hard in order to get the right sound. Once again we use our tonal coloration go-to plug-in—the BF76. There is a preset called Pump that should do the trick nicely. Set the input gain control so that the GR is around –7 dB. In this instance, we are controlling the dynamics, yes, but we're mainly after the *sound* you get by pushing the compressor. You may hear processing artifacts in the sound (pumping), but that can be considered secondary to the urgency and power that effect brings to the vocal performance. Find the balance of power/finesse that works with your mix.

Note: Keep your overall mix level averaging –12 dB on your output meter *before* you add the vocals. The vocals will add another 4–6 dB on top of the rest of the mix.

# Sculpting a Mix

Here's how you make a real sculpture:

**Step 1:** Get an enormous block of stone. Examine it and develop a concept of what the end product should look like.

**Step 2:** Chisel away large pieces of the stone to create the general shape of your sculpture.

**Step 3:** Using smaller/finer tools to refine the shape, smooth out the rough edges and create the subtler detail.

**Step 4:** Painstaking detail work. Sand and polish until perfect.

Note: It's important that you first develop an idea of what the final product will look/sound like. Just chipping away aimlessly will get you nowhere fast.

Here's how to apply the sculpting method to mixing:

**Step 1:** Start with a general blend of tracks; adjust all the tracks uniformly until the peaks on your Master Fader meter average between –12 and –6. You will want to leave some headroom room for any additive processing that might accumulate. Listen to the raw tracks and get a sense of their potential and where you want to take the mix.

**Step 2:** Make subtractive volume changes to each track as you see fit. Begin by turning down tracks that are too loud rather than turning up tracks that are too quiet. Place instruments within the stereo field based on your strategy for panning.

**Step 3:** At this point the mix should be taking shape, albeit a bit rough. Apply EQ and compression to further refine where each instrument sits in the frequency and amplitude domains. Use subtractive EQ to create room in the frequency domain for other instruments.

**Step 4:** Add the finishing touches to your mix. Use automation to finesse levels; choose reverb and effects to enhance the balance you've created.

Note: Soloing tracks is valuable at any stage in this process. Just be sure to A/B in context to keep a good perspective on how things fit together.

Thanks to James Nixon, a fine sculptor, for his help in defining this approach.

# Technical Aspects

## Dynamic Range

If you are recording in 24-bit mode in Pro Tools, the available dynamic range is 144 dB.

The Pro Tools host-based mixer runs at 32-bit floating point resolution, allowing you to sum the maximum number of tracks at +12 dB without clipping the mixer. You still need to use the Master Fader to trim the final output level to avoid hardware clipping, but it's good to know you have that kind of capacity.

HDX technology uses a 64-bit floating point mixer to yield over 1,000 dB of dynamic range on the mix bus. Headroom is an amazing +54 dB, yet the low-level resolution of this system is such that you can pull a fader down –90 dB and still maintain 24-bit resolution.

This means you are capable of mixing with detail and clarity at any amplitude level.

Use as much of that dynamic range as you can within the scope of the mix—don't just use the top 6 dB. Dynamic range is one of the things that made vinyl LP releases sound so good and have so much emotional impact. Loud was *loud* and soft was soft. Popular music in the 2000s resides almost exclusively in the top 3 decibels of the peak meter. That doesn't leave much room for subtleties. We'll discuss dynamic range more in the second portion of this book, looking closely at the mastering process.

### Bus Compression in Mixing

Consider using a bus compressor if you need it. How will you know if you need it? If your mix sounds right to you but the level is low on average, you may need to use a bus compressor to bring up the overall level without clipping the Master Fader. A single-band compressor deals exclusively with level and dynamic range control. The bus compressor can also tend to make your mixes "gel" better, though this is entirely subjective. By controlling the dynamic range, you are also making decisions about coloring the overall sound of your mix. Experiment with different compressors to determine which will give you the results you need to hear in your mix.

A multi-band compressor will affect frequency content as well as dynamics. This can be useful as a tool to compensate for deficiency or overabundance of frequencies in specific bands.

If your music will be mastered, either by you or someone else, be conservative in your use of multi-band compression. The goal is to make your mixes well balanced and even, and applying too much multi-band compression can make it harder to match levels and frequency response in the mastering stage.

Choose your weapons carefully.

## Gain Structure

Be aware that every gain-dependent device—whether it's hardware or software, EQ or dynamics, or even reverb and delay—has a cumulative cascade affect on your overall level settings. You should be sensitive to over-modulating or clipping any component in the signal chain. Distortion in the digital realm is not a pretty thing to behold, sonically speaking.

*Gain* is the term we use to describe signal amplification. There can be positive gain (e.g., +3 dB) or negative gain (–3 dB), or unity gain (0 dB).

In the audio world we use the term *unity gain* to describe the relationship between signal processing components in which gain is neither added nor subtracted in the process. If at every gain stage you calibrate settings so that there is no increase or decrease in signal volume or voltage as signal passes through, it can be said that you have achieved unity gain.

Why is this important? Because you can start with 0 dB and end with 0 dB but make one heckuva mess out of things in the middle. Here's an example. If I use a mic pre-amp that outputs 0 dB into a Pro Tools input channel, I would expect that the channel would record and output 0 dB, right? Right—so far so good. Now if I were to use a hardware insert to send a stereo mix signal from a Pro Tools Master Fader to an outboard compressor, it would arrive at 0 dB as well. But if in the process of compressing the mix I happen to adjust for –12 dB of gain reduction, then send it back to Pro Tools without compensation (or make-up gain), I have lost 12 dB of signal. The only way to make up that gain is to add another gain stage and boost 12 dB, thereby raising the noise floor by 12 dB, or to raise the Master Fader level +12 dB, thereby using up all of the available headroom, increasing the noise floor, and risking over-modulation from any peak transient that might make it past the outboard compressor.

In this example, we may have started with 0 dB and ended with 0 dB, but we also lost gain, added gain, and needlessly added noise and (potentially) distortion along the way. If we had observed the law of unity gain at every gain stage in the signal path, we would have avoided the problem entirely.

The bottom line is to: a) calibrate your devices, and b) watch your levels.

## Frequency Response

You should adopt a commonsense approach to EQ, meaning that you should only use EQ if a track needs it or if you're rectifying a problem.

Try to use subtractive EQ first, then resort to additive EQ if that doesn't yield the desired result.

Use the smallest EQ plug you can to get the job done. By smallest, I mean the one using the least amount of CPU cycles. For example, if you are only applying a High Pass Filter (HPF) to a vocal track, use the 1-band EQ 3 plug. It uses far fewer system resources than the 7-band EQ 3.

This practice will help manage your CPU resources and give you more processing headroom when you need it. Like when you are mixing 60+ tracks with lots of virtual instruments.

Try to avoid using multiple EQ plug-ins on the same track, unless there is a specific effect you're going for that can't be achieved by any other means.

Hint: Insert a spectrum analyzer plug-in on your Master Fader to keep an eye on the overall frequency response of your program.

## Metering

Pro Tools track meters show you the level of the signal after the final gain stage or plug-in. Here's why this is important to note:

The track meter does not show you the signal level as recorded, but only the level after processing, so you will need to insert another meter as a plug-in in order to check your processing gain stages for clipping. Yes, the clip light will glow on an offending plug-in if there are more than three consecutive clipped samples, but that doesn't always tell you if there's distortion present or where that might be happening.

The meters read the output level of the track as related to the fader, even after processing. This is known as post-fader metering. Good for reference, but if your plug-ins are all clipped and the fader is down at –24 dB, your track meter will not show your signal as clipping.

When in doubt, always solo and listen to the track for distortion.

Note: I tend to insert extra meters on my Master Fader if I'm adding more than one plug-in. That way I can keep track of each gain stage before it hits the output. Usually, I'll start with an RTA in the first slot to measure the unprocessed mix bus, then a multi-band compressor, then another RTA, and finally a TL MasterMeter or vertical Dorrough meter for precision.

This allows the user to meter and compare signal at three different points in the chain. Note: Pro Tools now offers different metering types! If you are using Pro Tools 11, you'll have your choice of four. If you're using Pro Tools 11 HD, you have seventeen. The examples I explain here are all using the "Pro Tools Classic" metering type, found in both versions of Pro Tools.

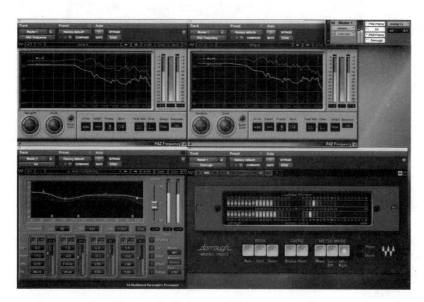

## Mixing to a Digital File

### Bounce to Disk

In Pro Tools you can create a mix file by using the Bounce to Disk command. This can be found in the Edit menu or can be initiated with a key command by pressing Option + Command + B. This will bring up a Bounce dialog that looks like this:

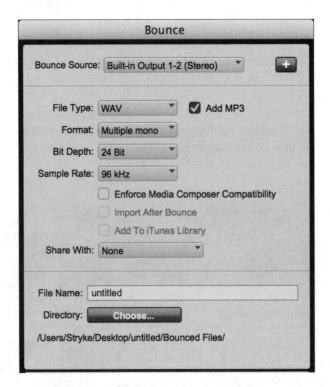

From here you can choose the destination file format, the source outputs that will feed the mixdown, bit depth, sample rate, and stereo (or multitrack) configuration.

If you plan on mastering your mix in Pro Tools, you should use the following settings:

- WAV file format
- 24-bit
- 88.2 or 96 kHz
- Multiple Mono files

Notice that next to the file type, there is a check box to create an MP3 file of your bounce. If you check it, an MP3 will be created, along with your chosen file format. You now need to name your file in the File Name box. Pro Tools will now automatically save all bounced files to a bounced files folder in your session folder. You can override this by clicking on the Choose button under the File Name box and direct Pro Tools to save your bounced files wherever you like. Please note: Wherever you decide to have your bounce rendered to, you should probably have *all* of your mixed audio files from the session there. Next, checking the Offline check box will allow your file(s) to be bounced faster than real-time—up to 150 times faster, depending on how many tracks and plug-ins you have in your session. Once you hit the Bounce button, your file will begin rendering. If you chose to render an MP3 as well or chose MP3 as your bounce source, a window will pop up before the bounce, which will allow you to tag your MP3 with the pertinent metadata for artist, track title, genre, and so forth. Note: If you are using Pro Tools HD, you will have the ability to do up to 16 multi-stem bounces as well!

# Mixing Summary

### Mixing Is Hard Work

**Optimize:** Optimize your computer system, audio hardware, and Pro Tools software to make your mixing session go more smoothly.

**Strategize:** Start with a strategy for mixing:
- Building the house
- Sculpting

**Goals:** Define your goals:
- Is this a demo?
- Is this for CD release?
- Will this be distributed electronically?
- What's the timeline for completion?

**Calibration:** Tune your ears by listening to mixes that sound great to you.
- Listen to these reference materials before you start your mix.
- Import full-fidelity mixes into your DAW for comparison to your own mixes.

**Work it:** If it sounds great right away, there's something wrong:
- In other words, it takes a lot of work to make a mix sound *right*. It will take substantially more than 15 minutes to create a great mix.
- It takes 90 percent of the time to finesse the last 10 percent of a mix.

**Practice:** Don't be discouraged if your mixes don't sound like Chris Lord-Alge the first time.
- Practice makes perfect.
- Repetition makes you better.

**Vocals:** If you have lead vocals, do your first mix with vocals balanced at just the right level.
- Then do an alternate mix with the vocals up +1.5 dB.
- Next, do an alternate mix with the vocals down –1.5 dB.
- Listen to all three; then decide which sounds best.

**Quality:** When you have arrived at the perfect mix, burn a CD and listen to it in your car.
- Next, listen to it on headphones.
- Then put in your earbuds, go for a walk, and listen to it.
- Next, listen on a friend's sound system.
- Finally, if it sounds good everywhere else, listen to it on headphones once again, and take note of every little noise or clunk or breath that you don't want on the master. Now go back and fix those problems and repeat this entire listening sequence.

# Preparing Your Tracks for Mastering

If you are sending your mixes out to be mastered by a mastering engineer, you should have a conversation with them to cover these questions:
- How long will it take?
- How much will it cost?
- Should I attend the mastering session?
- File Resolution: Do they want 16-bit/44.1 kHz files or 24-bit/96 kHz files?
- File Format: Multiple mono files or interleaved stereo files? WAV, AIFF, or?
- Delivered on hard disk, CD, DVD, hard drive, or tape?

- What about adding bus compression or EQ to the mixes before I deliver them?
- What level should I aim for: peaks of –12 dB, or 100 percent modulation? Somewhere in between perhaps?
- Your mastering engineer will guide you through the answers to these questions and more, and you will learn a great deal from them about the mastering process.

# Summary of Key Commands

| Operation | Key Command |
|---|---|
| Select Outputs on Multiple Tracks | Shift + Option + Click on Output Pane |
| Bounce to Disk | Option + Command + B |

# Chapter 6 Review

1. The two mixing methods described in this book are _____ and _____.

2. When building a mix from the foundation, you can usually start from the drum tracks and work your way up through the instruments by _____.

3. Instruments that are to be mixed in groups, like drums, can be controlled together by assigning them to a group. The quick way to assign a group is by highlighting the names of the tracks and pressing _____ + ___.

4. You can use Track _____ to apply software plug-in processing to _____ tracks, ____ inputs, _____ tracks, and _____ faders.

5. Applying EQ to drum tracks should be done on the individual track _____, rather than on a sub-mix.

6. Kick drums and bass guitars often share the same frequency range, usually between ___ and ____ Hz. You can use the _____ plug-in to shape the sound of each instrument to make room in the spectrum for both, thereby clearing up the low end.

7. Operating Pro Tools in 24-bit mode gives you a theoretical dynamic range of ____ dB.

8. Observing the law of _____ means making sure that your audio I/O is calibrated, and that at each gain stage no gain is added or taken away. This includes plug-in inserts as well as hardware inserts.

9. You should use the most CPU-economical plug-in to do the job. When inserting a high-pass filter on an audio track, use a ____-band EQ 3 plug-in to conserve system _____.

10. Pro Tools track meters display the _____ gain stage before output. In order to accurately measure the difference between amplitude as recorded and amplitude as processed, put a meter in the _____ position.

11. The command for Bounce to Disk is _____ + _____ + ___.

12. From the Bounce to Disk menu you can choose audio file format, _____, _____, and mono or stereo file format, as well as _____ source and conversion options.

# Chapter 7
# MASTERING OVERVIEW

**A**lso referred to as a type of *audio post-production*, mastering is the final step in the production process when preparing your mixes for distribution or duplication. The main idea is to optimize the sound of music mixes for playback on a wide array of sound systems, and in a variety of media ranging from vinyl LP to CD to compressed data file formats.

The way I describe it to my mastering engineers is like this: I give you a bunch of good mixes, you give me back a cohesive *album*.

Whether you are mastering for yourself or for a client, you should go into a session with fresh ears and an objective view toward achieving the best possible sound quality.

## What Does a Mastering Engineer Do?

**Quality Control:** The main task of a mastering engineer is to ensure that a song (or collection of songs) has sonic integrity and adheres to generally accepted professional standards.

**Critical listening:** A mastering engineer needs to be able to listen clearly, make objective evaluations, and determine what process or processes to employ in order to adjust the audio for best sound translation.

The mastering engineer will use software and hardware tools to manipulate dynamics and apply corrective EQ to the mixes in order to achieve this goal. In the case of a CD or vinyl release, the mastering engineer will also establish an appropriate amount of time between songs and ensure that there are proper fade-ins and fade-outs on each song, with no unwanted count-offs or end-of-take chatter to mar the listening experience. In general, an experienced mastering engineer will apply as little processing as possible in order to achieve the desired outcome.

## When Do You Need Mastering?

Almost always, if the goal is to have your music played on a wide array of playback devices and sound systems.

## You Should Have Your Music Mastered If

- Your mixes were done by different engineers.
- Your mixes were done in different studios.
- Your mixes were done at different times.
- Your tracks were recorded in different sessions at different times or feature different players.
- Your mixes come from a variety of media or file formats.

In the case of a compilation, you should have your completed project mastered if the songs came from different albums or artists.

## Should You Master Your Own Mixes?

It depends on the circumstances. In practice, by the time you're done mixing, you are often too close to the project to make truly *objective* qualitative decisions about the EQ or dynamics, especially after days, weeks, or months of making highly *subjective* qualitative decisions. Besides, if you mix a song to the best of your abilities, there should be no room for you to improve upon it, right?

An exception would be in the case of extreme budget limitation. If you own your own Pro Tools rig, it can definitely be more cost-effective to take on the mastering step yourself. Though it's often worth the added expense to get a pair of educated and objective ears on your mixes.

Bob Ludwig, one the top mastering engineers in the world, has an important view of this aspect of the process:

> With the record industry in a state of entropy and with similarly declining budgets, many producers and artists are forced to attempt to master their own music. It is said that it takes 10,000 hours of learning to master one's craft, which is why most of the world's greatest mixers (who spent their 10,000 hours learning how to mix) do not master their own work.

Note: I would encourage engineers to try their hand at mastering; it's a valuable experience. It's an informative process and will facilitate understanding the full scope of completing a recording. You never know—you may be good at mastering and really enjoy doing it.

## Thinking Like a Mastering Engineer vs. a Mixing Engineer

It's hard to separate yourself from the recording and mixing process, but a mastering engineer has to listen more objectively and in relative terms. It means finally letting go of the snare drum sound or the vocal reverb sound, or even the balance between the background singers. It means listening for surpluses or deficiencies in the frequency spectrum of the mix (too much of this, too little of that), then finding the proper EQ and/ or compression settings to compensate.

To that end, conduct the mastering session separately from the mixing process. Make sure that you are objective enough to make judgment calls on EQ or compression or overall level.

A mastering engineer should be concerned with making all of the songs in a collection sound like they belong on the same album, or at least were recorded by the same artist.

Grammy® nominated engineer David Miles Huber masters his own mixes in 5.1 surround, but he does it as a separate session after the mixes are completed. David imports his mixes into a new session and applies processing as necessary to maximize the sonic quality of his work. We will build on this approach as we create our mastering session.

# Basic Mastering Tools

The tools available to you in the mastering process are similar to the tools used in mixing, but they are used somewhat differently. These are:

- Volume-Based effects
- Time-Based effects
- Reconstructive Tools

## Volume-Based Effects

While you can't change the volume of each individual instrument in a song that's already been mixed, you can adjust the overall volume of a song, a portion of a song, or a group of songs in the mastering process. You can also fade in or fade out as a transition into or out of a song. You can also adjust the EQ characteristics of a song or a portion of a song, depending on the desired effect. Again, the main idea in mastering is to give the overall impression that the songs in an album sound similar to one another in relative level and EQ.

## Time-Based Effects

These would include phase modification tools, stereo enhancement, delay, and reverb. On rare occasions it may be necessary to add reverb in the mastering session, but if the mastering engineer noticed a problem in the mix (i.e., reverb on only one side of the stereo field, or a phase problem with reverb return), he or she would probably refer the mix back to the mixing engineer to be remixed.

It would be rare to add delay in the mastering stage, but more unusual things have happened.

## Reconstructive Tools

These include noise reduction, hum removal, hiss removal, and pop/click removal software. These are typically available as DAW plug-ins but often act as stand-alone software applications as well.

# Mastering in Pro Tools

## What You *Can* Do In Pro Tools

- Sequencing
- Adjust levels, fades
- Fine-tune EQ and compression
- Edit top and tail, edit length
- Determine overall and relative levels
- Remove noise
- Bounce each song as a master file

## What You *Can't* Do in Pro Tools

- Burn to CD or DVD
- Create or edit PQ sub-codes
- Check a CD master for errors

## Pro Tools in the Mastering Suite

Gateway Mastering in Portland, ME, uses four Pro Tools systems; this from owner Bob Ludwig:

> We often use a hybrid of analog and digital processing in our mastering as we still receive many analog tapes, and we also will go from the digital domain to analog and back in order to use unique pieces of analog gear and to get some sound colors that are only available in the analog world.
>
> It used to be that we rarely used any plug-ins on Pro Tools because the sound quality did not measure up to stand-alone digital hardware, but this situation has been rapidly changing. With the advent of powerful processing cards and boxes offered by Waves APA, Universal Audio's UAD-2 Quad DSP board, TC Electronic's *PowerCore FireWire*, and other accelerators, the DSP power of most outboard digital gear can now be had within the Digital Workstation and all the good things that it implies (automation, AudioSuite, etc.). Some of the new digital modeling of classic analog gear sounds very close and often offers more flexibility than the original units.
>
> We aren't entirely there yet; some stand-alone digital hardware like the Weiss DS-1 de-esser or the Weiss EQ1-LP linear phase IIR equalizer have massive latency in order to do the amazing things they do. Their native latency is far beyond the longest delay times Pro Tools can compensate for. Still, there is no reason not to believe that sooner rather than later most massively DSP intensive devices will be made available for Digital Audio Workstations, so the future is obviously heading towards all DAW processing.

## DIY Mastering in Pro Tools

Start with the Final Mixes: If you are mastering your own mixes, be sure that you are using the latest and best-sounding mixes for your project. If you have followed the file-naming conventions as discussed in the mixing part of this book, you should be able to easily locate and identify the latest versions of each mix.

Import audio at a high resolution.

Depending on the final destination, Pro Tools mastering sessions should be created according to the following specifications:

**CD Mastering—24-bit/88.2 kHz:** Use this setting for making a Red Book (audio disk) CD master, as well as for making audio files for web distribution.

**Mastering for Visual Content—24-bit/96 kHz:** If you are mastering audio for video, whether DVD or a video for social media distribution, use the 96 kHz sample rate.

Even if your final destination is 44.1 kHz or 48 kHz, your mastering session sample rate should use the higher multiple of the destination sample rate to make best use of the higher-resolution signal processing afforded the higher sample rates.

The common thinking here is that the conversion from 88.2 to 44.1 kHz—or from 96 to 48 kHz—is a simple mathematical division by 2, not some odd rate conversion from 96 kHz to 44.1 kHz, or 44.1 to 48 kHz, or some other number. While there is some debate about whether or not modern computers can handle that odd-rate math conversion without sonic artifacts, it makes sense to err on the side of being conservative with regard to the quality of your final audio.

Why not use 192 kHz sample rate? Mainly because audio convertors are not as accurate at that high rate of processing and may actually introduce distortion. This may not be as relevant in mastering as in recording, but if you are planning to use hardware inserts to perform external processing with analog gear, you will definitely be passing through several AD/DA conversion stages.

Also, audio files at 24-bit/192 kHz take up a lot of disk space, data bus throughput, and CPU processing horsepower, and don't necessarily yield additional *usable* frequency response (remember, we can only hear up to 20 kHz, approximately).

## Building a Mastering Session

Build a session with a new track for each song.

You will be able to customize plug-ins and signal path for each song, depending on what you think it needs.

This gives you the opportunity to experiment with different sequencing options, cross-fades, and more—without disrupting settings on other songs or modifying edits or fades.

## Assembling Tracks

Determine the running order and assemble songs/tracks in that order from top to bottom.

If you are mastering more than one song, this makes for a good visual representation of your running order and how songs flow together.

If you decide to change the running order, you can easily drag tracks around to rearrange the sequence.

## Monitoring

Compare your mixes, your mastered mixes, and your reference material often.

Use the solos to hear each track. On processed tracks, you will need to bypass plug-ins in order to hear the original mix without processing. Compare to your selected reference music to keep a good perspective on the sound of your mastered audio.

Calibrate your playback system for 85 dBC. Use this as your average listening level, but vary the level from time to time in order to avoid listening fatigue.

Be sure that you are using well-balanced speakers that allow you hear the low frequencies down to at least 30 Hz, or you may be missing a large portion of the information in that octave.

## Signal Chain

- Assign metering *first* in the insert chain on each track, including the Master Fader.
- Any plug-ins you add should appear after the meter, giving you an opportunity to keep an eye on levels pre- and post-processing.
- Add another meter at the end of the signal chain to observe your final levels.
- Experiment with EQ and dynamics plug-ins and the order in which they appear. There may be subtle differences in the outcome of each process, and you should be aware of what each option does to your audio.
- Construct your Window Layout scheme so that you can see all processing and metering at the same time on the desktop.

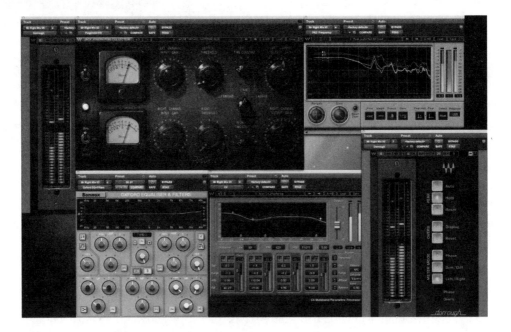

## Using Level Automation

Once you have arrived at a good dynamic and EQ balance, you may find it necessary to balance overall level from cut to cut. You can use the Level Fader to accomplish this, but if the level needs to change within a song, you can use the level automation to draw in the appropriate levels. These levels can be easily adjusted or modified and stored with the session for immediate recall.

## Dynamic Range Control

In the mastering stage, compression is used to fine-tune dynamic range and is generally most effective when added in small increments.

## Parallel Compression

Sometimes called "New York" compression, this refers to adding compression in such a way that allows you to hear both the compressed and uncompressed signal at the same time.

This can be useful when you want to compress a mix heavily to bring up the energy and volume level but still want to hear some of the dynamics and peak transients.

Some plug-ins, such as Maxim, utilize a mix control allowing you to determine the balance between compressed and uncompressed signal directly from the plug-in window. If you are using a dynamics plug-in without this feature, or wish to use an external compressor to accomplish this, use these steps to set up parallel audio processing:

**Step 1:** Click the Send button of the audio track to which you wish to add parallel compression. Select "new track . . . ," create a stereo Aux Input named "SongNameComp," and click Create.

**Step 2:** Set the Send level to 0 dB by Option + Clicking the fader.

**Step 3:** Assign a compressor plug-in to the new Aux Input and adjust to taste. Add other processing on the Aux Input as necessary or desired.

**Step 4:** Adjust levels on the "SongName" and "SongNameComp" track level faders to achieve the right balance between uncompressed and compressed audio.

## Serial Compression

Since inserts cascade in a series, adding a compressor as a plug-in on the audio track will compress the source audio as well as any processing that comes before the compressor plug-in.

## Using More Than One Compressor on a Track

It may be necessary to use more than one compressor when you need to control particular transients independent of the overall compression effect.

If some instruments in the mix are particularly peaky (high attack transients), set the first compressor in the chain to process with a fast attack, fast release, then set GR to taste.

Insert a second compressor to bring up overall level and smooth out dynamics using a longer attack time, longer release time, and reduce gain by no more than 2 or 3 dB.

## Multi-Band Compression

The Swiss army knife of the mastering realm.

We have discussed multi-band compression in at least two other places in this book. In the context of mastering, we need to look at multi-band compression as a powerful tool to accomplish sonic restoration as well as sonic enhancement.

It is important to consider how to set the variable crossover points to be used in dividing frequencies for independent processing:

**Low–middle band:** Crossover between the low-band and mid-band should be somewhere below the range of your lead instrument or vocal. Try crossing over at 200 Hz or below; otherwise, your processing may interfere with mix balances. For example, imagine if the crossover point were 500 Hz—smack in the middle of the vocal range; the singer's lower notes might be boosted along with the kick drum, while the middle and higher notes might be attenuated with the rest of the mid-range. Not a very realistic way to treat a mix.

**Middle–high band.** Again, setting this crossover relative to but *above* the range of the vocal or lead instrument will preserve the balance as intended in the original mix. A crossover setting of 3–4 kHz would put you out of the vocal range but still enable you to control the upper mid-range tendency to be strident.

## Restorative Use of Multi-Band Compression

I had a client bring in a mix that sounded like the drummer paid for the session—the snare was easily 6 dB louder than anything else in the mix. As it turns out, the drummer *was* sitting next to the mix engineer coaching him through his first mix in his new basement studio.

By using a multi-band compressor with one band tuned specifically to respond to the narrow-band center frequency of the snare drum sound, we were able to reduce the gain of that band by −6 dB for just the few-hundred millisecond duration of the snare hits. This reduced the volume of the snare enough to make the mix usable.

## EQ

Application of EQ will be to taste, but you should listen to your reference recordings again to hear the optimal balance between low, middle, and high frequencies. Then try to match the approximate balance between frequencies using your EQ.

Note: In raising particular high-frequency bands, be careful not to turn the recording into a high hat song. By changing the EQ balance to bring out vocal breathiness, for example, you might alter the delicate balance achieved in mixing the rest of the instruments.

## Create a Master Fader

This gives you an opportunity to add an overall compressor, EQ, or other processing to the cumulative output of your session.

Used sparingly, and using a very high quality limiter can really make the sound of your tracks more cohesive at this stage.

The Master Fader also gives you a method for trimming final volume up or down, and for metering your final output.

## Create A Pre- and Post-Processing Monitor Bus

If your audio interface has at least four outputs, and you have a mixer or the ability to switch monitor sources, you should create a separate monitoring path for A/B comparison of pre- and post-processing of your audio.

The setup is a bit more complex, but definitely more flexible in the long run.

**Step 1:** In your I/O page (Setup > I/O), create a new output path called "Solo Bus" and assign it to outputs A 3–4.

**Step 2:** Go to the AFL/PFL Path drop-down menu and select Stereo A 3–4 as the solo bus. This assigns the output of the solo bus to physical outputs 3–4 of your audio interface.

**Step 3:** In the AFL/PFL Mutes drop-down menu, select A 1–2. This mutes the main stereo output 1–2 whenever you hit a solo button. (Note: Remember this later; you'll need to set it to "none" when mixing.)

**Step 4:** For each audio track, click the Send button and create a new Aux Input named "SongName AUX." Set the send level to 0 dB (Option + Click on the Send fader). Set the output of each audio track to "no output."

**Step 5:** All of your processing and plug-ins will need to be inserted on the Aux Input that corresponds to each audio track. You can color code the track pairs (e.g., "SongName" and "SongName AUX") to make them easier to identify.

**Step 6:** Now, soloing the "SongName" track will output the unprocessed signal to your I/O 3–4 outputs for instant A/B comparison listening without having to turn off each plug-in individually. Just be sure to calibrate the 1–2 and 3–4 outputs to the same volume level.

Note: Be sure to bounce your files to disk using the A 1–2 outputs in order to hear and print the files with signal processing.

## Overall Level Optimization

Listen to the transitions repeatedly, and listen to the entire collection of songs from beginning to end to be sure that the levels from song to song, and the overall level of the project, are well balanced and appropriate for the style of music you are mastering.

Even though a ballad may have been mixed with peaks of –1 dB, that doesn't mean it should appear at that level in context with other songs.

Likewise, though a pounding rock song may have been mixed with peaks of –12 dB, that does not mean it should appear that way in context either.

The only way to determine the appropriate relative level from track to track is by listening carefully from beginning to end, comparing all tracks.

## The Level Wars

Much carnage has been wrought in the name of loudness, beginning notably with the Metallica *Black* album. If you can, avoid the temptation to subscribe to the theory that louder is better when it comes to mastering. Again, Bob Ludwig:

> There are times an uneducated A&R person may reject a mix because they refuse to change their playback level, and mixes that are done with dynamic range and lower average levels are rejected out of hand. This unfortunate casualty of the Level Wars causes people to try to master their own work. Of course, Pro Tools offers many tools that a professional mastering engineer now uses, so some people think because they own a DAW they are now a mastering engineer. People need to do what they need to do, but often the result is that otherwise good engineers actually damage the musicality of their own work. Instead of making it more musical, they merely make it louder. This is a crime against art.
>
> If someone decides to "pre-master" their mixes before giving them to the artist to listen to, we prefer to be supplied both the "listening" mix and the original pre-squashed mix so we have something we can work with. It is a sad fact that once someone puts a very loud, squashed reference out in the world, many people's knee-jerk reaction is to prefer this louder version without evaluating what damage is being done to the musicality. They don't stop to consider the human body's proven hearing physics that are trained to "tune out" stimuli (music) that is static and without dynamics.

## Checklist Before Printing Final Bounces

- Establish final running order
- Fine-tune all timings and transitions between songs or tracks
- Create fades as necessary
- Set beginning and end points for each song file to be bounced
- Check all levels to be sure there are no digital clips or "overs"
- Check level song by song and in context overall
- Double-check to be sure all your plug-ins are active and that all external processing devices are powered-up and connected
- Document all external processor settings to keep track of revisions
- Make sure that your track output routing is set to your main stereo outputs
- Check your hard drive to be sure you have enough space for the bounced files

## Bouncing Your Mastered Files

- Triple-check to make sure all appropriate tracks are un-muted and un-soloed, and that all your plug-ins are active.
- In the Edit window, select the START marker of your first song, then Shift + Click on the END marker, creating a clip selection within the timeline.
- Choose the Bounce menu (Option + Command + B), and create a new folder on the same disk as your sequences. Name the folder "MyProject Mastered Mixes."
- For CD masters, create 16-bit/44.1 kHz AIFF files.

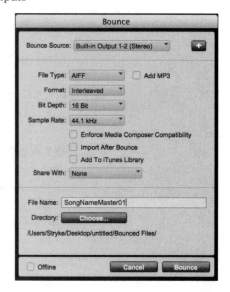

- For DVD or video-bound content, create 16-bit/48 kHz AIFF or WAV master files. Check with the author or editor of the project for any additional specs.
- Some video projects have very specific audio level requirements, particularly if they are destined for television broadcast.
- Film projects may require delivery of stems, or stereo sub-mixes of your tracks. Be sure to ask for these specs before completing your mastering.
- Name the bounce "SongNameMaster01" and click OK.
- You should monitor the bounce carefully to be certain everything sounds right, to detect errors, and to be sure the bounce content and length is correct.
- Repeat this sequence for each song or track.
- When completed, you should have all of your final mastered and bounced files located in one folder, properly named, and easily identifiable.

## Creating the Final Master CD

You can use any third-party program to burn a master CD. Follow these steps:

**Step 1:** Open a new session in your CD authoring software, name it "MyProject CD Master01" and save it to the same disk directory as your mastered mix files.

**Step 2:** Drag all your mastered mix files into the session and put them in the proper running order.

**Step 3:** Remove any default timing gaps between tracks. Because you established the precise running times of each track on your Pro Tools mastering session, you will not need any gaps between tracks.

**Step 4:** If there is an option for entering metadata into the CD authoring directory, now is the time to populate those fields. Include disk name, ISRC codes, artist, publishing and copyright information, and any other information pertinent to project identification.

**Step 5:** Burn two master disks. If you have a client, burn three disks.

**Step 6:** Listen to each, checking for errors. In particular, check for phase coherence in mono.

**Step 7:** Seal one copy and set it aside for duplication. Set another aside as the client reference copy, if applicable.

**Step 8:** Use the remaining copy to check *very carefully,* listening end to end using headphones. Check for quality on a variety of systems before sending any copies to the duplicator or the client.

**Step 9:** Once this CD passes all of your listening tests, you can mark or label each of the disks as *masters* and feel relatively confident in sending the remaining copies to their respective destinations.

Any CD listening or reference copies can be made directly from one of the CD masters.

## Do I Need to Master My Music for MP3 Distribution?

Usually not. Some distributors require a specific format, but they will usually tell you what they need or can convert the files themselves. There is no obvious reason to master specifically for MP3 files, as you can easily rip them from your master CD at any data rate required. Just be sure you have preserved some dynamic range in your mastered tracks.

## Documentation

Keep meticulous notes on all of your processes and file names; create a text document and include it with your mastered files for future reference or from which to prepare revisions.

If your CD authoring program is capable of exporting an edit list with P and Q subcodes, save that as a text file with your mastered files as well. The duplication plant may request a copy of this document along with the master disk.

## Delivering a Master for Duplication

Send the clearly labeled, unopened master CD to the duplication plant, along with the printed PQ subcode list. Include all information about the project that you can supply. Most manufacturers have a stringent submission process that identifies the information needed before they accept projects.

In some cases a duplicator may accept hard drives, DVDs, or specialized DDP files. Check with your duplicator of choice for its delivery specifications.

## Delivering a Master for Online Distribution

Different distributors may ask you to encode files into a specific format at a specified data rate, or for a CD from which they will generate their own files.

Aggregators usually ask for both uploaded files and market-ready CDs for physical distribution. Again, check with your distributor of choice to determine its deliverables.

## Backup vs. Long-Term Archival of Your Data

When everything has been mixed, mastered, and delivered, it's time to think about storing your data.

### Backup

Data backup is considered a short- to medium-term solution for storing data, and usually involves transfer to hard drive, CD-R, DVD-R, BluRay, or other optical media. These formats are not designed for long-term storage, but will suffice for three to five years.

Hard drives are designed to last up to three years, per manufacturer standards, and then only if exercised (mounted) every three months or so.

Optical media is not designed for long-term storage, regardless of manufacturer claims.

Be prepared to migrate your data to newer formats about every three to five years.

Refer to the "Backup" section earlier in this book for references to P&E Wing Backup guidelines.

### Archival

There was a statement earlier in this book: "Data isn't data unless it lives in three places." That means three different physical formats in three different physical locations.

Professional data tape storage is considered to be the standard of choice for enterprise-level IT departments.

Exabyte tape is the standard of choice for the Library of Congress, in addition to immediate online access via enormous RAID servers.

Some institutions still rely on analog tape for reliable long-term storage. When you consider that tapes from the 1950s still exist—and are playable—it speaks highly of the longevity of the technology.

Again, you should refer to the P&E Wing document relating to Archival and Delivery Standards for professional audio projects.

# Mastering Summary

- Treat mastering as a separate process once mixing is completed.
- Often we are too close to our own work to be objective about the sound. Take some time off between mixing and mastering, and listen to your other reference material to gain perspective on your ideal frequency response target.
- Determine how loud your songs need to be compared to others in the market. Compare your reference music to your levels.
- Use other mastered projects as aural reference. Pick several examples in a similar genre that sound right to you.
- Run through the pre-bounce checklist before you bounce final files.
- What's the final destination format? If this project is destined for CD, you'll need 16-bit/44.1 kHz AIFF files. If this is destined for DVD or video, you'll need 16-bit/48 kHz AIFF or WAV files. If this is for online distribution, your distributor will tell you what it needs.
- Bounce all your files to the same folder, named appropriately.
- Create more than one CD master; don't send the duplicators the one with fingerprints all over it!
- Make sure you back up your files.

# Summary of Key Commands

| Operation | Key Command |
|---|---|
| Set Fader Level to 0 dB | Option + Click - Fader |

# Chapter 7 Review

1. The _____ session should be created as a separate session for mixing, as you will be using different processing and signal _____.
2. The three basic tools used in mastering are _____-based, _____-based, and _____ tools.
3. Pro Tools as a mastering platform allows you to sequence tracks, adjust _____ and _____, and apply processing, but does not allow you to burn a ____ or _____ directly from the program.
4. Create a new Pro Tools session for mastering using the data rate of ___-bit/_____ kHz for mastering a CD, and ___-bit/___ kHz when mastering for video.
5. _____ should be the first plug-in on audio tracks, including on the Master Fader.
6. The two ways to use compression in mastering are _____ connection of compressors, and _____ compression, a.k.a. "New York" compression.
7. When bouncing mastered songs, the file format should be ___-bit/_____ kHz AIFF for CD and MP3-bound projects, and __-bit/_____ kHz AIFF for video projects.

# In Closing

I hope this book helps you to make better music. At the very least, I hope that you are inspired to practice your craft and keep your learning curve vertical.

Keep studying, read up on new technologies and old processes.

Until next time—work hard, play hard, and keep getting better!

# Frequency Chart

Here is a graphic that will help illustrate the spectrum of human hearing as it relates to both frequency in Hertz and the range of various instruments in relation to the piano keyboard. Use this as a guide to identifying frequencies contained in musical performances.

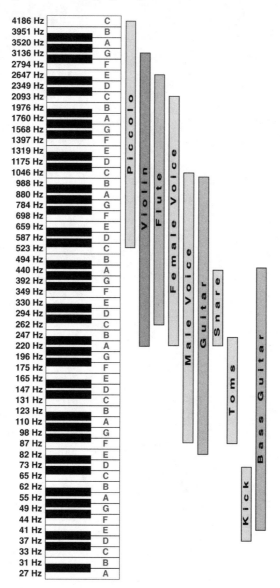

# APPENDIX: ONLINE VIDEO TUTORIALS AND PRO TOOLS SESSIONS

## Video Content

The accompanying video tutorials demonstrate the concepts and techniques explained in *Mixing and Mastering with Pro Tools 11*. The featured sessions were recorded in an earlier version of Pro Tools that used the term "region" when referring to sections of audio and MIDI data on the timeline and tracks of the edit and arrange windows. Pro Tools 11 now calls these audio and MIDI sections "clips."

The online video tutorials contain extremely valuable tips and technique. Use them to help get the most out mixing and mastering audio with Pro Tools 11.

Videos 1–3 introduce you to the world of Pro Tools.

Videos 4–6 discuss screen layout, basic operation, and editing functions.

Videos 7–12 show how to effectively configure the virtual mixer in order to mix, automate, and render a final product.

Videos 13–15 explain the mystery of mastering, and they summarize the mastering process.

### 1. Introduction
Welcome to the world of Mixing and Mastering in Pro Tools.

### 2. Launching Pro Tools
Understanding how to open existing sessions or create new ones is the first step in Pro Tools proficiency. This segment shows:

- The proper order for powering up a system
- Where to store audio and session files
- How to efficiently manage the DAW from the first mouse click

### 3. How to Use the Session Files
Copying tutorial material from their online location to your hard drive, opening sessions, and keeping track of data is important to your learning experience and to your workflow. This tutorial helps ensure that you don't lose your assets!

### 4. Edit/Mix Window Layout
Getting around in Pro Tools is easier when you understand the window layout. This tutorial will guide you through the:

- Edit window
- Mix window
- Top menu bar
- Edit modes

## 5. Transport Functions

Pro Tools navigation is simple and elegant, yet has many configuration options for customizing the creative work environment. This segment focuses on:

- Counters and status displays
- Record options
- Playback options
- Creating and managing markers
- Creating custom Window Configurations

## 6. Data Management

This tutorial digs deep into the best ways to get data in and out of Pro Tools. It demonstrates methods to easily create and locate templates, mix versions, session files, and more. Overviews of these important functions are included:

- Import audio
- Import session data
- Export as AAF/OMF
- Bounce to disk

## 7. Building a Virtual Mixer

Pro Tools lets the user configure a mixer so that it provides exactly what's needed to mix each song. Explore the various tools available to design the ideal virtual console and see how to use that design as a starting place for future mixes.

## 8. Using Direct Plug-ins

Plug-ins are fundamental creative building blocks in the development of virtually every mix. This video demonstrates the use of plug-ins, inserted directly on a recorded track, to control dynamics, adjust EQ, and control pitch.

It also shows the differences between—and recommends some uses for—serial and parallel processing. This segment helps you avoid some of the biggest (and most common) processing mistakes made by beginning DAW users.

## 9. Using Auxiliary Inputs

Whether adding reverb to tracks or creating a headphone mix, the auxiliary input is a very powerful weapon in the mixing arsenal. Learn to maximize flexibility and minimize system resources using aux busses.

## 10. Automation

Pro Tools offers an automation system that is easy to use, yet very powerful. This tutorial gets you started using automation quickly and effectively.

## 11. Bus Processing

Turn a good mix into a great mix just by inserting some simple processing tools at the end of the mix chain. See how bus processing with dynamics or EQ adds a bit of polish to the overall sound of your mix.

## 12. Creating the Final Mix File

Take a step-by-step look at the process of bouncing your final mix to disk. This video demonstrates output options for Pro Tools and provides important considerations regarding the creation of files that are suitable for the mastering process.

## 13. Setting up the Mastering Session

Mastering is the final step in the recording process. Once you're proficient at building a virtual mixer and using plug-in processing, you can use those concepts in a slightly different way to create a mastering session.

## 14. Creating Mastered Song Files

Finally! You've made it through the mixing and mastering process and it's time to bounce your final mastered song files. This tutorial walks through options for the creation of files that will be uploaded to a digital distribution service or burned to a CD for duplication.

## 15. In Closing

This video segment contains final comments from the author.

# Audio Content

The three Pro Tools sessions used in these video exercises are available online They provide an opportunity to get some hands-on experience using professionally recorded multitrack masters! Use them to explore the vast array of tools and techniques available to Pro Tools power users.

# ANSWER KEY FOR CHAPTER REVIEW QUESTIONS

## Chapter 1

1. a. Volume-based, b. Time-based, c. Spatial
2. Loudness, EQ, dynamic range control
3. Time-based effects
4. spatial effect, short delay
5. recording studio
6. speakers, control room, system
7. Intel
8. all of your computer's available
9. FireWire, USB 2.0
10. day
11. 3
12. MIDI, Ethernet
13. Near
14. 2, headphones, car stereo
15. 85
16. fatigue
17. 24
18. 88.2

## Chapter 2

1. Pro Tools
2. delay, I/O
3. iLok
4. monitoring, HD
5. AAX, PCIe, HDX
6. DSP
7. Usage, power
8. host-based
9. High, AAX
10. N, I/O
11. internal, external
12. S/PDIF, ADAT
13. I/O Settings
14. Shuffle, Slip, Spot, Grid
15. Zoomer, Trim, Selector, Grabber, Scrubber, Pencil
16. Smart
17. mousing/clicking, key command

# Chapter 3

1. -2.5 dB, -3 dB, -4.5 dB, -6 dB
2. signals, routing
3. Pre, post-fader
4. plug-ins, I/O device, external processing
5. voice
6. serial
7. Reverb, sends
8. Option + Drag
9. delay, hardware
10. 10, 10
11. Master Fader
12. dithering
13. digital noise
14. HDX
15. a. Comments
    b. Inserts
    c. Sends
    d. I/O assignments
    e. Track Color
16. tempo, meter
17. Edit, Mix
18. m , . /
19. Enter, 999
20. Command + S

# Chapter 4

1. file, effect
2. Avid Audio eXtension
3. 10
4. Control + Command + Click
5. You don't. You'll have to use one of the standard pull-down menus.
6. AudioSuite, Aux
7. EQ
8. 1, 4, 7 band
9. subtractive, additive
10. False
11. limiting, compression
12. frequency bands
13. 10:1
14. sibilance
15. pitch change, auto pitch-correction
16. Phase reverse
17. delays
18. AIR Dynamic Delay, AIR Multi Delay, Mod Delay III

19. time-based
20. distortion
21. Beat Detective
22. Stereo

# Chapter 5

1. Volume, Pan, Mute, Send level, Send pan, Send mute, Plug-in parameters
2. Off, Read, Write, Touch, Latch, Trim
3. Command + 4
4. automation enable
5. overwrite
6. thin
7. auto, automation lanes
8. Trim

# Chapter 6

1. Building a House, Sculpting
2. frequency spectrum
3. Command + G
4. Inserts, audio tracks, aux inputs, instrument tracks, master faders
5. insert
6. 50 and 100 Hz, EQ 3
7. 144 dB
8. Unity Gain
9. one-band, resources
10. final, first insert
11. Option + Command + B
12. bit depth, sample rate, output source

# Chapter 7

1. mastering, flow
2. volume-based, time-based, reconstructive tools
3. levels, fades, CD or DVD
4. 24-bit/88.2 kHz, 24-bit/96 kHz
5. Metering
6. serial, parallel
7. 16-bit/44.1 kHz AIFF, 16-bit/48 kHz AIFF

# INDEX

16-bit, 41, 58, 86, 103, 113–114, 116,
192 kHz, 109
24-bit, 15, 40–41, 80, 99, 102–104,
    108–109,
44.1 kHz, 15, 86, 103, 108, 113, 116
48 kHz, 15, 23, 108, 114, 116
64-bit, v, 2–3, 12, 19, 59, 99
88.2 kHz, 15, 102, 108
96 kHz, 15, 102, 103, 108

## A

AAF file format, 3, 17, 20
AAX plug-ins, v, vii, 2, 19, 42, 59–60,
    62, 67–68, 73
        Native, vii, 2, 28, 59, 67
        DSP, vii, 2, 60, 123,
Absolute Grid mode, 25
acoustics, v, 10–11, 14, 95
acoustic guitar, 65, 95, 97–98,
acoustic piano, 96–97
active
    insert, 35
    send, 39
    track, 40
AFL/PFL path, 112
Aggregate I/O, v, 2, 17–18, 21–22
AIFF file format, 15, 86, 103, 113–114,
    116
Algorithm, vii, 41, 43
all tracks, 44, 54
alternate playlists, 53
ambience, 9
amplifier, 14, 55, 90
amplitude, 42, 55, 63–64, 67, 90, 92, 95,
    98–99
analog, 9, 13, 19, 23, 31–32, 38, 41–43,
    80, 82, 108–109, 115
analog console, 13, 31–32, 38, 42–43,
    80, 82
Antares Auto-Tune, 68
archival, x, 13, 59, 113
arrangements, 7–8, 70

arranging, 84
artifacts, 98, 108
ASIO, 17–18, 22
assignments
    bus, 23, 112
    group, 33, 38, 44, 54
    input, 24, 29, 41, 112
    insert, 26, 36, 38, 60, 72, 109
    output, 23–24, 29, 33, 38, 40–41, 112
    send, 24, 26, 33, 38–41
attributes, 33
audio clip, 25, 27, 37, 59, 62, 68, 89
audio file format, 5, 15, 102, 103–105,
    114–116
audio interface, 2, 17–20, 22–23, 28,
    40, 112
Audio Suite, vii, 23, 59, 62, 68, 71, 73,
    108
audio track, viii, 2, 18–19, 23, 25, 31,
    34, 36–38, 40, 42, 46, 55, 62,
    75–76, 79, 82, 89, 110–112, 116
audition, 23, 77, 93
Audition Path, 23
authorization, 17–18, 20
Automatic Delay Compensation
    (ADC), 17, 22, 37, 60, 62
automate, viii, 13, 64, 68, 71, 75–76, 78,
    82, 88, 94
automation
    Auto Join, 77
    Auto Match, 77
    Auto Safe mode, viii, 78, 98
    capture, 8, 77–80, 82, 91
    editing, viii, 25, 68, 78–79, 82
    enabling, viii, 77, 80
    Join, 77
    parameters, viii, 25, 44, 68, 76–80, 82
    plug-in, viii, 3, 13, 35, 76, 78, 80, 82, 96
    Preview Mode, 77
    thinning automation data, viii, 79
    undo, 79
automation modes
    Latch, 77
    Off, 76

Read, 76
Touch, 77, 80
Trim, 77, 80
Write, 77, 79
auxiliary input (aux)
    aux sends and returns, vii–viii, x,
        18–19, 24, 31, 33–34, 36, 38, 40–42,
        58, 62, 70–71, 76, 88, 110, 112, 120
AVID, v, vii–viii, xiii, xv, 1–3, 6,
    12–13, 17–20, 26, 28, 59–60, 63,
    66–68, 70, 72, 80

## B

backups, 12, 85
bandwidth, 86, 96–97
bars/beats, 24
bass, ix, 8, 14, 43–44, 55, 62, 64–65, 69,
    84, 90, 93–95, 97, 104
bass frequency, 14, 43, 64, 90, 93–95,
    97, 104
Beat Detective, 71–72
bit depth, 15, 102
bounce, v, x, 2–3, 50, 59, 62, 101, 102,
    104, 107, 112–114, 116, 120–121
Bounce To Disk, 3, 50, 101, 104,
    112–113, 120–121
breakpoints, 25, 78–79
buffer settings, vi, 21, 28
bussing, x, 13, 17–20, 23–24, 31, 33,
    36–38, 41–42, 58, 62, 66, 88–89,
    99, 101, 104, 109, 112, 120
BWAV file format, 15
bypass, v, 3, 34–35, 42, 57, 60, 64, 94,
    109

## C

C|24, viii, 13, 80
cache size, vi, 22
calibration, vi, 18–20, 113
capture, 8, 77–80, 82, 91
channel strip, 42, 47
chorus (effect), 9, 69–70, 73
chorus (arrangement), 4, 50, 84–85
click track (metronome), 46
clip list, 23, 27, 85

clips, vii, 3–4, 23–28, 35, 37, 40–41,
    45–49, 51, 55–57, 59, 62, 68,
    71–73, 77, 79, 85, 87, 89, 93–94,
    113
clipping
    clear clip indicator command, vii, 35,
        40–41, 73
clock source, vi, 22–23, 28
color palette, vii, 47, 87
compression, viii, x, 9, 13, 62, 64,
    66–67, 71–73, 83, 86, 88, 93–95,
    97–99, 104, 106–107, 110–111,
    116
computer
    CPU, 20–22, 36, 56, 70, 89, 100, 104,
        109
    interface, 3, 12
    Mac, 4, 5, 12, 17–19, 22, 28
    PC, 5, 12, 15, 18, 22, 25
    processor, vi, 12, 15, 21
    RAM, 1–2, 12, 20, 22, 59–60,
    requirements, 12
    system settings, 1
conductor track, 46, 53
console, vi, ix, 9, 10, 13, 31–32, 38,
    40–43, 63, 75, 80, 82, 84, 120
consolidate clips, 56, 85
control surfaces, vi, viii, 13, 15, 77, 80,
    82
copy command, 36, 44, 57, 61, 72
Core Audio, 17–18, 22
count-off, 53, 88, 105
current engine, 21
Cut command, 56–57

## D

DAE, v, 2
data management, ix, 85, 120
DAW, ix, xiii, 1, 3–5, 9, 41, 53, 62,
    75, 82, 86, 103, 107–108, 113,
    119–120
dB, 9–10, 14–15, 20, 32, 36, 40, 43,
    64–67, 77, 90–91, 93–101,
    103–104, 109–112, 116
decibel, 10, 99
de-esser, viii, 62, 64, 67, 73, 108

delay, viii, 2, 3, 9, 15, 19, 22, 33, 36, .37–38, 67, 69–70, 72–73, 99, 107–108

delay compensation, vi, 17, 22, 37

dialog, 22–24, 26, 28, 35, 40–41, 48, 52, 55, 101

DigiBase, 17

Digidesign (Digi), v, xiii, 1, 2

digital, v, ix, 1, 9, 13, 22–23, 41, 43, 58, 60, 71, 99, 101, 108, 113, 121

Digi User Conference (DUC), 1

disk allocation, vi, 23

display
    edit window, vii, x, 5, 25–27, 34, 38, 43–48, 50, 52–53, 58, 60, 73, 78–79, 82, 87, 89, 113, 119
    HEAT, vii, 41–43, 58
    insert status, 35
    markers, vii, 44, 47–48, 50, 53, 58, 120
    rulers, 44, 48, 58
    send status, 39
    system usage, 20–21, 42
    tracks, 38, 44–45, 47, 58, 79

distortion, viii, 8, 14, 41–43, 71–72, 90, 97, 99–101, 109

dither, vii, 41, 86

drums, ix, 43–44, 50, 54–55, 87–88, 90–92, 97, 104

DSP, vii, 2, 19, 21, 40, 42, 60, 108

duplicating tracks, vii, 54

duration, 25, 55–56, 70–71, 111

dynamic processing, vi, 2, 13, 22, 62, 84, 92–93, 95–96, 110, 120

dynamic range, viii, ix–x, 8–9, 62, 66, 92, 94, 99, 104, 110, 113–114

Dynamics 3 plug-in, 66–67, 92, 94, 96


**E**

Edit commands, 27, 33, 44, 46, 79, 82

Edit modes
    Grid, vii, 24–25, 46, 50, 58, 72, 79
    Shuffle, 24, 46
    Slip, 24
    Spot, 24

Edit tools
    Grabber tool, 25–26
    modifier keys, 22, 25
    Pencil tool, 25–26, 79
    Scrubber tool, 25
    Selector tool, 25–26
    Smart tool, 25–26
    Trim tool, 25–26, 71
    Zoomer tool, 25

Edit window, vii, x, 5, 24–27, 34, 38, 43–48, 50, 52–53, 58, 60, 73, 78–79, 82, 87, 89, 113, 119

editing, vii–ix, 4, 24–27, 29, 32, 44, 46, 49, 51, 53, 55–56, 64, 68, 71, 78, 82, 84, 89, 93, 119

Elastic Audio, 22, 72

electric guitars, 64, 93, 95–96

Eleven plug-in, 71, 90

EQ, viii, x, 3, 9–10, 13, 35–36, 60–65, 69–71, 73, 80, 84, 90–91, 93–100, 104–107, 109–112, 120

equalization, 9, 43, 63, 71

equalizer, 63–64, 108

EQ 3 plug-in, 35, 63, 67, 73, 90–91, 95–96, 104

Ethernet, 3, 13, 81

EuCon, viii, 80–82

expaansion, 9, 19, 67, 71–72

export, v, 3, 17, 115, 120

external clock source, 23


**F**

fades, 14, 25, 40, 107, 109, 113

fader, vii–viii, x, 33–34, 38, 40–41, 43, 49, 58, 76–77, 80, 82, 97–101, 104, 109–110, 112, 116

file format
    AAC, 86
    AIFF, 15, 86, 103, 113–114, 116, 125
    BWF (WAV), 15, 102–1–3
    MP3, 3, 14, 86, 102, 114, 116
    WMV, 86

File menu, 5, 85

final mix, x, 108, 121

FireWire, 12, 108

flanger, 70

folders, 5, 23, 85, 102, 113–114, 116

format
    clock source, vi, 22–23, 28

session data, v, 3, 5, 15, 43, 52, 57
stereo pan, vii, 32, 58, 72
frequency, 14, 36, 41, 58, 73, 93, 95–96,
104, 106, 109, 116

**G**

gain, 3, 20, 40, 64–67, 93–96, 98–101,
104, 111, 119
gain structure, ix, 4, 99
gates (gating), vii–viii, 9, 55–56, 62, 67,
73, 94, 96
Grabber tool, 25
Grid mode, 24–25, 46, 50
Grid settings, viii, 46, 50, 58, 72, 79
groups, vii, 26, 28, 32–33, 44, 47, 49,
54, 78, 82, 87, 104
guitar
acoustic, 65, 85, 95, 97–98
amp emulator, 71
dynamics processing, 93, 95–96
effects, 62, 71, 90, 95–96
electric, 64, 93, 95–96
EQ, 64–65, 95–96
gating, 55, 96
naming conventions, 85
submix tracks, 62

**H**

H/W Buffer, 21
H/W Insert Delay, 37–38
hard drives, vi, 5, 12–13, 15, 18, 85,
103, 113, 115, 119
hardware inserts, 9, 19, 33–34, 37–38,
58, 100, 104, 109
Hardware Setup menu, 22, 37
harmonic, viii, 42–43, 66, 71, 97
HD, vi, 2–3, 17–21, 28, 41, 75–77,
101–102
HDX card, 19, 21, 28
headphones, 7–8, 14, 33, 103, 114
Heal Separation, 55, 57, 93
HEAT, vii, 41–43, 58
hiding tracks, 45, 58
high-pass filter, 95, 98, 100
Hill, Dave, 41

host-based, 21, 59, 99
Host Engine, 2, 21, 68
Host Processors menu, vi, 21
Huber, David Miles, 106

**I**

I/O Settings, vi, 17, 22–23
I/O Setup, 18, 21–23, 37
ignore errors, 21
iLok, vi, 11, 17–18, 20, 28
Import Session Data 3, 5, 43, 52, 57,
120
inactive
inserts, 34, 57
plug-ins, 35, 60, 73
sends, 40
tracks, 45
input, viii, x, 2, 5, 20, 23–24, 26, 28,
31, 33–34, 37–38, 40–41, 58, 62,
66–67, 71, 73, 76, 80, 88, 92–93,
98, 100, 104, 110, 112, 120
insert, vii, 3, 9, 19, 24, 26, 33–38, 42, 44,
57–61, 67, 71–73, 80, 82, 89–91,
100, 104, 109, 111
instruments, ix, 2, 8–10, 18, 31, 33,
43–44, 55, 59, 65, 69–72, 85,
87–88, 90–91, 93–98, 100, 104,
107, 111, 117
Instrument tracks, 18–19, 31, 34, 38, 42
interface, 2–3, 9, 12, 17–20, 22–23, 28,
40, 112

**J**

Join command, 77

**K**

key commands, vi–x, 3, 5, 12, 22,
25–28, 53, 57–58, 72, 82, 93, 101,
104, 116
keyboards
Keyboard Focus, vi, 26–28
Clip List, 23, 26–27, 85
commands, vi, 27–28
Group List, 28

Keyboard Focus access, 28
key input, 38, 67
kick drum, 8, 14, 55, 62, 64–65, 87, 90–94, 104, 111

**L**

Latch automation mode, 77
latency, 2, 17, 21, 28, 60, 108
Level Wars, x, 8, 113
limiting, viii, 66, 92
low-frequency band, 63–67, 87, 90
low-pass filter, 63
Ludwig, Bob, xv, 106, 108

**M**

Mac, 4–5, 12, 17–19, 22, 28
Make Inactive command, 34–35, 45, 57, 60, 73
Markers, vii, 44, 47–50, 53, 57–58, 113, 120
Master Fader, vii–viii, x, 34, 40–41, 43, 49, 76, 98–101, 109, 112, 116
mastering, ix–x, xiii, 2, 4–5, 8, 11, 20, 41, 43, 67, 86, 99, 102–116, 119, 121
Melodyne, 68, 73
Memory Location window, 48, 50, 53, 57
Memory Locations, vii, 47, 49–50, 53, 57
Menus, 5, 21–26, 28–29, 32, 35–38, 40–41, 44–45, 48, 50–52, 56–57, 59, 61, 73, 79, 82, 85, 88, 101, 104, 112–113, 119
meter, v, ix, 3, 20, 35, 38, 40–42, 44, 49, 72, 93, 97–101, 104, 109, 112
metronome, 46, 53
microphones, 8, 69, 73
MIDI, viii, 13, 18–19, 24–25, 27, 31, 46, 53, 76
mix busses, 17, 19, 33, 99, 101

mixing, v, ix, xiii, 2, 4–5, 7–8, 10–13, 15, 20–21, 24, 28, 31–32, 36, 41–44, 51, 53, 62–64, 66, 69–71, 75, 79–80, 83–84, 86–87, 96, 98–101, 103–104, 106–108, 111–112, 116, 119–121
Mix window
monitoring
    mid-field, 14, 90
    near-field, 14
mono, 8–9, 32, 36–38, 40, 62, 69, 89, 102–104, 114
MP3 file format, 3, 14, 86, 102, 114, 116
multi-band compression, viii, x, 67, 99, 111
multi-channel, 7, 41
multi-mono, 36
muting, 32, 35, 38–39, 45, 55–57, 60, 76, 79–80, 88, 112

**N**

New Group command, 44, 57
New Memory Location dialog, 48
New Track command, 41, 57
"New York" compression, 110, 116
Nixon, xv, 99
noise reduction, 107
notch filter, 63–64, 91
Nudge settings, viii, 46, 58, 89
nudging, vii, 9, 46–47, 57–58, 89, 93
Numeric Keypad, 32, 48, 50, 53, 57–58

**O**

OMF file format, 3, 17, 120
Options, 2–3, 22, 26, 35, 38, 44–45, 48, 52–53, 61, 87, 120
oscillator, 37, 62
outboard gear, vi, 9, 13, 19, 84, 108
outputs, 3, 5, 17, 23–24, 29, 31, 33, 36–38, 40–41, 45, 58, 62, 66–67, 71, 80, 88–89, 92, 94, 97–102, 104, 112–113, 121
overdubs, 11, 60
overhead mics, 87, 89

**P**

pan, vii, 9, 25, 32, 38, 58, 69, 72–73, 76, 79, 93, 95–98
parallel compression, x, 97, 110
Paste command, 57, 61, 72
pasting, 44, 57, 61, 72, 79
paths, 23–24
PC, 5, 12, 15, 18, 22, 25
PCI/e cards, 19, 28, 60
Pencil tool, 25–26, 79
peripheral devices, vi, 3, 18, 22
phase, 8, 69–70, 73, 107–108, 114
phaser, 70
piano, 97, 117
pitch tools, viii, 62, 68–70
platforms, xiii, 1, 3, 12, 62, 75, 116
playback, 2–3, 11–14, 21–22, 25–28, 43, 59–60, 77, 79–80, 82, 84, 105, 109, 113, 120
Playback Engine, vi, 21–22, 28
Playlists, vii, 53–54, 77–78
plug-ins, v–viii, x, 2–3, 5, 9–11, 13, 15, 17–22, 26, 28, 31, 33–38, 41–42, 55–56, 58–63, 67–73, 76, 78, 80, 82, 89–92, 94–98, 100–104, 107–113, 116, 120–121
plug-in settings, vii, 61, 72
post-fader, 33–34, 38, 40, 100
pre-fader, 33–34
preferences, 47, 79, 81
printing effects, vii, 59, 62
processor, vi, 12, 15, 21, 38, 92, 113

**Q**

QuickTime, 5

**R**

real-time, vii–viii, 2–3, 13, 20–21, 38, 44, 55, 59–60, 62, 68, 72, 76, 80, 102
reverb, viii, 3, 9, 15, 24, 33, 36, 38, 41, 55, 58, 70, 73, 98–99, 106–107, 120
Revert to Saved command, 93
rulers, 44, 48, 58

**S**

sample rate, vi, 15, 18–19, 22–23, 102, 108–109
Save As command, 5
Save Copy In command, 85
saving, 53, 59, 89
Scrubber tool, 25, 123
Selector tool, 25–26, 123
sends, vii, 31, 33, 38–40, 44, 58, 71
serial compression, x, 111
sessions, ix–x, xiii, 2, 5, 7, 23, 31, 52, 85–86, 106, 108, 119, 121
settings, vi–vii, 1, 3, 5, 17–18, 20–23, 28, 31–32, 36, 43, 46, 49–50, 52, 58–61, 66–67, 70, 72, 77, 79, 86, 90, 99–100, 102, 106, 109, 113
Show/Hide tracks, 49
Shuffle mode, 24
side-chain, vii, 62, 94
signal flow, 4
signal path, 100, 109
Slip mode, 24, 46
Smart tool, 25–26,
Smooth and Thin Data, 79
Snapshot, 77
Snap To commands, 24–25
soloing tracks, 99
spatial effects, v, 8–9
Spot mode, 24
stereo, 5, 7–9, 14–15, 24, 32, 36, 38, 40–41, 58, 62, 69, 72, 86, 88–90, 98, 100, 102–104, 107, 110, 112, 114
stereo bus, 38
stereo pan, vii, 9, 32, 58, 72
stereo tracks, 62, 88–90
Strip Silence, vii, 51, 56–57
sub-clip, 55, 72
sub-menu, 26, 35
surround, 5
system settings, 1, 20
System Usage window, vi, 20–21, 42

**T**

take, 45–47, 53, 56, 85, 88, 105

tape, 42–43, 70, 103, 108, 115
TDM, 2, 43
TCE, 72
templates, 31, 120
tempo, 4, 44, 46, 53, 70, 72
threshold, 55, 66–67, 94, 96
thinning automation data, viii, 79
time-based effects, viii–ix, 8, 36, 69–70, 107
time code, 17, 24
time compression, viii, 71–72
timeline, 5, 25, 37, 48–49, 59, 103, 113
timing, 24–25, 46, 55, 69, 71–72, 89, 93–94, 113–114
toggling, 26, 44
Touch automation mode, 77
Track List, 40
Track Name, 40, 44–45, 47, 54–55, 61
tracks
    view or hide tracks, 45, 49
transients, 67, 89, 92, 94–95, 97–98, 110–111
transport, x, 53, 57, 77, 82, 120
Transport window, vii, 46, 53
trigger, 55, 67, 94
Trim tool, 25–26, 71
tuning, 68–69, 73

**U**
Undo command, 47, 50, 57
unity gain, 99–100
USB, 18, 20, 28

**V**
video, v, x, 2–3, 5, 12, 15, 18–19, 42, 82, 85, 108, 114, 116, 119–121
video files, 3, 85
View menu, 48
Views, 49, 52–53, 79
view selectors, 53, 78–79, 82
virtual instruments, 2, 18, 31, 59, 72, 100
voices, 8, 19, 21, 34, 45, 60, 62, 73
volume, 7, 9–10, 14, 25, 32–33, 40–41, 55, 62, 73, 76, 92, 95, 97–98, 100, 107, 110–112
volume-based effects, ix, 8, 15

**W**
WAV file format, 15, 102, 114, 116
waveform, 23, 25, 56, 71, 78, 89, 93
website, 1, 5–6, 12, 18–19, 59, 86
Window Configuration, vii, 49–53, 57
Window menu, 26
windows
    opening multiple send and insert windows, 40
Word Clock, 22
Write automation mode, 3, 77

**Z**
zooming, 25, 37, 49, 89, 93
Zoomer tool, 25

# CREDITS

The musical examples used in this book and online media are from a song by the amazing and wonderful Keely Whitney:

Mr. Right

©2010 KeelBop Music Publishing

Lyrics by Keely Whitney

Music by Keely Whitney and Barry Aiken

From the forthcoming album "Untold Stories" by Keely Whitney

http://keelywhitney.com/

Used with permission